'A fresh and practical approach to managing anxiety. Through relatable examples and a compassionate, friendly tone, this book provides evidence-based strategies that empower individuals to make impactful changes in their daily lives. I highly recommend this guide for anyone looking to take control of their mental health.'

Professor Trudie Chalder, *Professor of Cognitive Behavioural Psychotherapy, King's College London, UK*

'At the height of a mental health crisis this book is an essential blueprint for all young people, equipping them with the tools they need to live a calmer life with less suffering... This is an inspiring, young, and wise perspective on anxiety. I cannot recommend it highly enough.'

Claire Dale, *author of the award-winning book* Physical Intelligence – Harness Your Body's Untapped Intelligence to Achieve More, Stress Less and Live More Happily

'This book is a concise and beautifully written guide to understanding and managing anxiety. In a voice that is relatable, warm, and insightful, it provides its reader with manageable, evidence-based strategies to improve their mental health. It's one I'll be recommending to all!'

Dr Imogen Bacon, *Medical Doctor (BMedSci BMBS)*

Outsmart Anxiety

Outsmart Anxiety: A Practical Guide to Understanding and Empowering Your Mind offers readers a comprehensive and compassionate exploration of anxiety, providing the tools to navigate their own experience with confidence and clarity.

With Felton's friendly and relatable voice, complex concepts are broken down into clear, practical insights that explain what anxiety is and why it arises. Through real-life examples, personal stories, actionable tips, and evidence-based strategies, this book blends professional expertise with genuine experience to create an accessible and empowering guide.

Ideal for teenagers, young adults, parents, teachers, and mental health professionals, *Outsmart Anxiety* serves as an essential toolkit to deepen understanding of anxiety and develop self-awareness—whether for oneself or in supporting others.

Lily Felton is a trainee clinical psychologist with a background in psychological research and a passion for making evidence-based tools accessible. She combines clinical insight with empathy to help readers navigate anxiety and build resilience in everyday life.

Outsmart Anxiety

*A Practical Guide to Understanding
and Empowering Your Mind*

Lily Felton

Routledge
Taylor & Francis Group

LONDON AND NEW YORK

Designed cover image: © Adobe Stock Images

First published 2026
by Routledge
4 Park Square, Milton Park, Abingdon, Oxon OX14 4RN

and by Routledge
605 Third Avenue, New York, NY 10158

Routledge is an imprint of the Taylor & Francis Group, an informa business

For Product Safety Concerns and Information please contact our EU representative GPSR@taylorandfrancis.com. Taylor & Francis Verlag GmbH, Kaufingerstraße 24, 80331 München, Germany.

Trademark notice: Product or corporate names may be trademarks or registered trademarks, and are used only for identification and explanation without intent to infringe.

British Library Cataloguing-in-Publication Data
A catalogue record for this book is available from the British Library

ISBN: 978-1-041-13506-7 (hbk)
ISBN: 978-1-041-13503-6 (pbk)
ISBN: 978-1-003-67011-7 (ebk)

DOI: 10.4324/9781003670117

Typeset in Optima LT Std
by KnowledgeWorks Global Ltd.

Access the Support Material: www.routledge.com/9781041135036

Contents

Acknowledgements

To my editor, Alice, thank you for your unwavering patience and your preparedness to respond to the most moronic questions fired over more frequently than I'd like to admit.

To my parents—who backed me wholeheartedly, despite my chronic lack of common sense. My sister and brother—neither of whom have read the book, and probably never will. To my boyfriend—best of luck finishing it by the time it comes out. I love you all despite the odds.

I would also like to express my gratitude to the following individuals and organisations for their generous permissions, valuable contributions and support throughout the development of this manuscript:

Figures

All figures have been designed and artworked by Roger Felton using royalty-free vector images from his Adobe Stock account.

Quotes

You can't control the wind, but you can adjust your sails.
Kristen Proby, *New York Times* bestselling author,
The Seymour Agency. Used with permission from
the Agency.

Avoidance is the best short-term strategy to escape conflict, and the best long-term strategy to ensure suffering.

Brendon Burchard, www.growthday.com, www.brendon.com, www.highperformanceacademy.com. Used with permission from Team GrowthDay.

Technology, with its promises of connection, can sometimes drive us deeper into disconnection and anxiety.

Sherry Turkle, *Alone Together*, copyright © 2010. Reprinted by permission of Basic Books, an imprint of Hachette Book Group, Inc. Used with permission from publisher.

Prologue

Everyone experiences moments in life when they feel overwhelmed, even when everything appears to be going well. I want to share a personal story that many of you might find familiar, one that illustrates just how unexpected and confusing anxiety can be.

The Surprise Reading Aloud

When I was in high school, I was always seen as a calm and composed student. However, one day, my English teacher announced that we would go around the room, and one by one, read a chapter from the book we were studying: 'Jane Eyre'. I remember my heart racing, my palms became sweaty, and I was engulfed by a surge of panic. I couldn't understand why I felt distressed over something so trivial. After all, I read all the time—so why was speaking in front of a few peers causing me such anxiety? I remember wishing I had the key to mastering it. That day, I learned that anxiety doesn't always make sense. Sometimes it comes out of nowhere and catches you off guard.

I later discovered that this feeling was more common than I had initially realised—and you know what? It was okay to experience it. It marked the beginning of my journey to understanding my own anxiety. Through much trial and error, I learned that anxiety isn't just something to be managed— it's something that can be **outsmarted**. I explored countless practical strategies and read more articles than I care to admit. Along the way, I realised I could take back the reins over my anxiety and transform it into a source of strength. In other words, I could beat it at its own game!

DOI: 10.4324/9781003670117-1

Fast forward a few years, I was faced with a new challenge: deciding whether to write this book. Ironically, it was anxiety that stopped me once again. Anxiety about what people would think, if I was knowledgeable enough, if anyone would even care. I can't say there was one defining moment that spurred me into action, rather an increasing realisation that I've tackled anxiety before and outsmarted it—so why not do it again, right? With my background in psychology, I felt fortunate to have the knowledge and tools to aid me in navigating it, and I hoped I could turn this challenge into another opportunity for growth. If I could just share what I'd learnt— even if it helps just one person—it would justify writing the book. So, fears aside, I hope that I can help as many of you as possible to understand your own mind a little better—especially if anxiety likes to crash your party too!

This book offers a clear, user-friendly guide to understanding anxiety: what it is, why it happens, and how to take action for yourself or others. It may also be valuable for the fortunate few who haven't faced significant anxiety but are looking to build their awareness.

I also want to answer the question WHY. All too often we are told to *'do more exercise'*, *'practise self-care'* or *'take up yoga'* to help protect our mental wellbeing, but no one ever tells us WHY. I hope this book will answer these sorts of questions, and consequently, encourage you to begin finding what helps you. The thing about anxiety is that you never know when it may affect you or someone you love. Having the knowledge and tools ready for when this happens can be very reassuring. After all, knowledge is power! In these pages, you'll find tips and tricks backed by science and personal experience that aim to reframe your relationship with anxiety from one of fear to one of authority. Each chapter builds on the previous one, helping you develop a toolkit for outsmarting anxiety and restoring your inner calm.

A Little Bit about Me

I'm a trainee clinical psychologist and, like most of us, I've met many people suffering with differing degrees of anxiety. In fact, anxiety has been one of the most prevalent issues within the mental health services I've worked in, from inpatient male wards to older people's community services.

We nearly all know someone who's struggling with their mental health (whether it's a family member, a close friend, or ourselves). Sometimes this is temporary—it's completely normal to feel anxious or low at times. Other times, these feelings can be overwhelming and have a profound effect on our daily functioning. That's when we need to check in with ourselves and others. That's when showing up can make all the difference. There have been plenty of occasions when I have utilised the contents of this book to support myself AND those around me in differing ways. I may not always do or say the right thing, but merely showing awareness, empathy and understanding of what someone else is going through can go a long way to help.

Throughout my years working within mental health services, I've seen a lot of misinformation surrounding common mental health problems, leading to a host of issues when it comes to implementing preventative and protective measures in a timely manner. I count myself among the fortunate for stepping into the mental health sector when it was becoming an increasingly acceptable topic of conversation, shedding its taboo status after being stigmatised for so long. Over the course of this time, I have gained a deep understanding of how humans perceive and interpret the world around us. Why we act and think in certain ways and the influence environmental factors have on human development and behaviour. I have learnt about different theories, debates and interventions to help people with varying presentations. All of which I hope to pass on to you in an understandable and digestible manner using real-life case studies and examples.

Perhaps the most important thing I have learnt on this journey is that everyone is completely and beautifully unique. As such, what proves beneficial for one person may not necessarily be effective for another. This can be incredibly liberating, depending on the way you view it! Within psychology, this concept is referred to as the 'no one size fits all' approach, which directs us away from viewing people as uniform and towards a more person-centred, holistic approach.

How This Book Can Help You

Now, this book doesn't claim to fix all problems associated with anxiety. Nor will it get close. Anxiety is a multifaceted phenomenon that cannot be described in its entirety within the contents of this book alone (nor in multiple books for that matter!). Rather, this book is about how to manage and understand anxiety, in the hope of making it that little bit easier to navigate the increasingly unpredictable world we live in.

This book is for you if you:

- Hope to improve your understanding and awareness of anxiety
- Want to equip yourself with useful tools and tips to help tackle anxiety (in yourself and/or others)
- Are looking for a friendly guide from someone with personal experience in managing anxiety

This book is NOT for you if you:

- Expect to be anxiety-free by the last page
- Are not willing to make some (simple) adjustments to your lifestyle
- Believe stress can be cured with binge-watching a marathon of puppy videos—although, to be fair, that does sound pretty tempting!

Throughout the book you'll find quotes and stories from ordinary young people as well as from various well-known public figures and professionals. There seems to be this idea that many famous people are untouchable, devoid of hardships. However, they struggle with their own mental health just as much as, if not more than, the average person (whatever average means!). I hope that sharing some of their journeys with their own anxiety can help dispel such myths and make you feel less alone with your thoughts. Anxiety doesn't discriminate, no matter how many world number one tracks or bestselling movies you release!

How to Use This Book

This book is designed so you can dive into the parts that matter most to you. Here's a quick look at how it's structured:

- **Introduction and History:** Kick things off with a quick introduction to anxiety and its background to set the stage.
- **Lifestyle Hacks:** Explore some simple, practical tips for managing anxiety through small lifestyle changes.
- **Mindfulness Exercises:** Try out some easy mindfulness exercises to incorporate into your daily routine.

- **Daily Tips for Stress:** Steal some handy tips to reduce stress on a day-to-day basis.
- **Supporting Others:** Learn how to spot signs of anxiety and be the best support buddy.
- **The Bottom Line:** Wrap things up with an overview of the most important bits and some pearls of wisdom from influential thinkers.

Feel free to jump to the chapters that catch your eye or align with your current needs. You don't have to read it all at once—just pick and choose what works for you, and when!

Want more? Additional worksheets and resources to support your journey can be accessed for free at www.routledge.com/9781041135036.

Before You Dive In: A Quick Note

I sincerely hope that this book resonates with readers as a supportive guide rather than a rigid manual pledging instant liberation from anxiety. I want individuals to lead happier lives, which, from my perspective, depends on the ability to achieve balance, consistency, and discovering what works best for them. So, without further ado, let's embark on this journey together and start outsmarting anxiety today!

You can't control the wind, but you can adjust your sails.
Kristen Proby, *New York Times* bestselling author

1 | The Uninvited Guest in Your Head

Why can't I just be NORMAL like everyone else?

Figure 1.1 A glimpse into my thoughts: a page from my personal journal.

Anxiety is a lot like a toddler. It never stops talking, tells you you're wrong about everything, and wakes you up at 3am.

Anonymous

> **GOAL:** Introduce anxiety as both a physical and mental response, clarify related terms, and highlight different types of anxiety.

1.1 Anxiety 101: Breaking Down the Jargon

Ever felt your heart racing before an exam, or sweaty palms just thinking about speaking in front of people? Congratulations, you've met anxiety! But don't fret—you're not alone, nor are you stuck with it. In this chapter, we'll take a look at what anxiety really is, why it shows up (usually at the most inconvenient times!), and the different flavours of anxiety there are. You'll also get to hear some real-life stories from people who have experienced anxiety before learning some powerful tools and practices to outsmart it. As we take the plunge, keep this in mind: **Let's get comfortable with the uncomfortable!**

DOI: 10.4324/9781003670117-2

Adopting this mindset will help you face anxiety with courage and curiosity, leading you towards your inner Zen Master. Stick with me, and you'll thank yourself later!

> *Sometimes I wonder if there is something wrong with me. Why is it that I'm stuck in my own head, overthinking Every. Single. Thing. Why can't I just be normal like everyone else? But then I heard the word 'anxiety', and it was like – oh. So, there's a name for this thing I'm feeling. I might not be broken after all…*
>
> Me

According to psychological literature, anxiety is an emotion characterised by feelings of tension, uneasiness, worry and fear. It commonly involves anticipation of future threats and often presents with physical symptoms like increased heart rate (American Psychiatric Association, 2022). But that's a bit technical. So, what does it actually feel like in real life? Let's hear it straight from the source. One of my friends, lets name him 'Tom', described anxiety as feeling like:

> *A constant hum in the background of my mind, making me second-guess every decision. Even when everything around me seemed fine, my body and mind were convinced something terrible was about to happen.*

Some anxiety is actually good for us. It is our brain's way of protecting ourselves from danger. You may have heard of the 'fight or flight' response, designed to help us survive by preparing us for potentially dangerous situations (we'll come back to this later).

We all experience anxiety at times in our lives—for example, before sitting an exam, as well as in relatively minor situations like missing an appointment or being stuck in traffic. This is totally normal and is called 'situational' anxiety and is not a disorder. Let's look at an example of this:

> *The night before a big job interview, Joe could barely sleep. His mind was racing with thoughts like, 'What if I mess up?' or 'What if they don't like me?' He worried about tripping over his words or blanking on a question. He felt nauseous and shaky when he got*

out of bed the next morning. His heart was pounding, and his hands were clammy. As he sat in the waiting room, every passing minute felt like an hour. By the time they called him in, he was so nervous that he could hardly focus on what the interviewer was saying. He kept thinking, 'What if they see how anxious I am?' He knew he was qualified, but the anxiety made it nearly impossible to think clearly or respond naturally.

Does the above example sound familiar to you? Situational anxiety is very common and is a very *effective* and *adaptive* function of the brain. It helps us manage and confront specific stressors, enhancing awareness and performance as well as boosting motivation and wellbeing (Brooks, 2014).

Following the previous example, here's a personal one that might resonate with some of you.

From Parental Guidance to Self-Guidance

The months leading up to starting university were filled with excitement and a sense of the imminent freedom I had been longing for. The only minor obstacle I had to navigate was figuring out how to get my mum to leave my dorm room while she cried endlessly about her 'baby leaving home'. The quicker I could get her out the door, the sooner I could get to my first freshers blow out. However, as the moving day approached, I began to feel increasingly worried. I had to manage my own laundry (which I had previously thought was only a parent's job) and make new friends. What if no one liked me and I was a complete loner? I wondered. All my excitement was overshadowed by fears of not fitting in or struggling academically. The night before the six-hour drive from my small, quiet village in southern England to the Angel of the North, I barely slept a wink – definitely not ideal, especially since I had imagined kicking things off with an all-nighter! If you asked my mum, she'd probably say I was a bit snappy during the drive, which I put down to my anxious jitters. Once I arrived, however, my anxiety began to dissipate and continued to ease as I gradually became acclimated to my new surroundings.

My experience is a reminder that feeling anxious during significant life changes, like starting university, is a universal experience. Stepping into the unknown can be daunting, but these feelings are a normal part of transitioning. Recognising these feelings and finding the right strategies to manage them—some of which you'll learn in this book—is the key to navigate this challenging period successfully.

Same same, but different: It's important to know that worry, stress and anxiety are related but different psychological states. Let's take a look at how to tell them apart:

Stress → in our body. Usually short-term and triggered by external factors
Worry → in our mind. Usually short-term and controllable
Anxiety → in our mind AND body. Usually persistent and disruptive

A bit of all of each of these states is actually good for us, but a lot of either/all can be harmful, regardless of our age. Research has shown that most of us have too much of all (Borkovec, Ray and Stöber, 1998).

In some instances, anxiety can be non-stop and significantly affect our daily life. This happens when our brain overestimates the threat in the environment by activating the 'fight or flight' response inappropriately, hence the mental 'worry'. This causes physical symptoms such as the heart racing and agitation. Essentially, the body and mind are on high alert. This may cause the adoption of maladaptive behaviours to perceived threats, for instance, avoiding social situations. For some people this can lead to what is called 'Generalised Anxiety Disorder' (GAD)—a disorder characterised by uncontrollable worry and anxiety, as well as physical symptoms like sleep disturbance and restlessness (American Psychiatric Association, 2013).

It is important to know the *why* before getting to grips with the *how* of managing yourself effectively. Once we understand why we experience certain symptoms, we are better placed to work out how best to fix them. Remember, knowledge is power!

As Prince Harry shared during the Heads Together *mental health campaign,* 'It's okay to not be okay.'

1.2 The Anxiety Squad: Worry's Different Personas

Paulo Coelho, author of Manuscript Found in Accra, *reflected that anxiety has been with us since the dawn of time, and since we have never been able to defeat it, we must learn how to live with it—much like living with the unpredictable nature of storms.*

There are several different flavours of anxiety—it isn't just one thing, so to speak. Within the world of psychology, these different types are outlined in a book about mental health and how to understand it, called the *Diagnostic and Statistical Manual of Mental Disorders* (5th ed.; DSM-5; APA, 2013). Let's take a quick look at some of the most common types as well as some examples to see how they may manifest:

Generalised anxiety: worrying all the time about everything and anything, e.g. constantly worry about job performance, finances and relationships, despite there being no immediate issue.

Social anxiety: worrying about what others will think of you, e.g. they will think you're stupid or boring. Take the following example:

The Assembly Hall Jitters

I remember in sixth form I had to stand up in assembly and give a speech about the hockey results. The thought of speaking in front of the entire school made me incredibly anxious to the point where I felt physically sick. I jumbled my words, and my hands shook as I held the paper. I remember feeling intensely embarrassed, with my inner dialogue convincing me that everyone was laughing at me and thinking I was an idiot. In the moments following the speech, I just wanted to blend into the dreadful wallpaper of the assembly room. But you know what? No one cared, and no one thinks about it now (except me, evidently!). The point is, we often stress over what others think of us, even though they seldom think about us at all—everyone's far too busy thinking about themselves! (Human beings are quite self-absorbed …)

Panic attack: sudden, intense episode of anxiety/fear that triggers physical symptoms (e.g. racing heart) without the presence of 'real' danger.

PRO TIP: If you think you are having a panic attack, No Panic offer a recorded breathing exercise to help regulate your breathing. Call **01952 680835** (available 24/7).

Phobias: an extreme, irrational fear of an object or situation, e.g. spiders, snakes, flying.

Let's look at a real-life example. This one's from the woman who brought me into this world, my darling Mum!

Cloudy with a Chance of Fear

Fear of flying, formally known as aerophobia, has plagued my mum's entire life. Just thinking about flying causes her extreme anxiety, making even short flights a challenge, let alone long-haul ones.

I remember a time in my teens when she bravely agreed to an eight-hour flight for a holiday. She had been preparing herself mentally for months, but her anxiety was so intense that she became physically ill in the week leading up to the flight—experiencing hot sweats, stomach pains and sleep problems.

On the flight, she started having palpitations and breathing difficulties, which led us to call the on-board doctor for assistance. After a few very tense hours, we made it to our destination, albeit not in one piece. She was unwell for most of the holiday and only began to feel back to normal several weeks after returning home.

This experience is just one example of how debilitating a phobia can be. It's no surprise that she has only been on only two flights since that trip.

PRO TIP: Visualise a positive outcome to boost your confidence before social occasions.

Actor Emma Stone publicly shared when she experienced her first panic attack while at a friend's house, where she was overwhelmed by fear. Although there was no real danger, the event was the beginning of three years of non-stop anxiety.

Brain Boost

Females are more likely than males to experience anxiety:

- Reproductive events such as pregnancy can cause hormonal fluctuations which have been found to contribute to higher rates of anxiety in females. This is also known as 'baby brain' (Russell & Lanius, 2013).
- Differences in brain chemistry cause higher rates of anxiety in females (McLean & Anderson, 2009).

This does **not** mean that anxiety in men is any less important, or that men with anxiety require less help or attention. Anxiety is anxiety, whoever experiences it. It's important to remember that it does **not** discriminate. If you need help, reach out. It's okay not to be okay.

Reflect & Act: Types and Tips

Reflect:
- Do you notice a specific type of anxiety most in yourself? (Generalised, social, panic, phobia?) Are there any specific situations that trigger this type of anxiety?

Act:
- Try counting slowly down from ten when you start to feel anxious. Remind yourself: *'This feeling will pass.'* Write down your thoughts so you can begin to identify patterns.

Key Takeaways

Before we move on, here's what to remember from this chapter:

- Anxiety impacts both our mind and body with physical and mental symptoms.
- Anxiety acts as our body's natural defence mechanism, protecting us from danger. Experiencing anxiety on an occasional basis is normal, but when it is excessive or chronic it can be debilitating.

- Situational anxiety can actually benefit us by boosting our motivation and wellbeing.
- Anxiety, stress and worry may all show up uninvited, but each brings its own punch!
- Anxiety comes in various forms, such as generalised anxiety, social anxiety, panic attacks and phobias, each of which comes with its own challenges.
- Females are more prone to anxiety than males, largely due to different in hormones and brain chemistry.

Mission accomplished: Anxiety Basics—Nailed It!

Next stop: The wonderful world of our brains—we're about to dive headfirst into how your brain ticks! Understanding how your mind works is key to giving your anxiety a run for its money. Ready to get the lowdown on your brain and flip the script on anxiety? Let's go!

References

American Psychiatric Association. (2013). *Diagnostic and statistical manual of mental disorders* (5th ed.). American Psychiatric Association.

American Psychiatric Association. (2022). *Diagnostic and statistical manual of mental disorders* (5th rev. ed.). American Psychiatric Association.

Borkovec, T. D., Ray, W. J. & Stöber, J. (1998). Worry: A cognitive phenomenon intimately linked to affective, physiological, and interpersonal behavioral processes. *Cognitive Therapy and Research*, 22(6), 551–563.

Brooks, A. (2014). The impact of anxiety on exam performance and learning: A review of the evidence. *Educational Psychology Review*, 26(4), 49–63.

McLean, C. P. & Anderson, E. R. (2009). Behavioural activation in the treatment of anxiety disorders: A review of the literature. *Behaviour Research and Therapy*, 47(8), 747–754.

Russell, G. & Lanius, R. (2013). Anxiety in females: The role of neurobiological and psychosocial factors. *Journal of Anxiety Disorders*, 27(2), 123–135.

2 Brain Frenzy
The Unplanned Roller Coaster

My brain isn't trying to ruin my life ~~completely~~ - its just doing its job.

Figure 2.1 A glimpse into my thoughts: a page from my personal journal.

> **GOAL:** Explore how anxiety comes from your brain's built-in survival response and how understanding it helps you manage stress.

The human brain is a very complex organ, containing more than 89 billion neurons (eek... that's a lot!), allowing us to think, learn, store (remember) and feel (Lent et al., 2012). It is the essence of who we are. There have been countless studies into the brain and there is still a long way to go before we get anywhere close to fully understanding it. Nonetheless, we do know some of the basics, which can help us understand how the cogs turn and what brain health really means. Don't worry, we'll keep it simple!

The amygdala is a small, almond-shaped part of the brain, known in the medical world as a small collection of nuclei (see Figure 2.2; Linsambarth et al., 2023). It plays a crucial role in protecting us against threat and processing our emotions and memory. Think of it as an advanced threat detection system. Basically, it's pretty amazing!

DOI: 10.4324/9781003670117-3

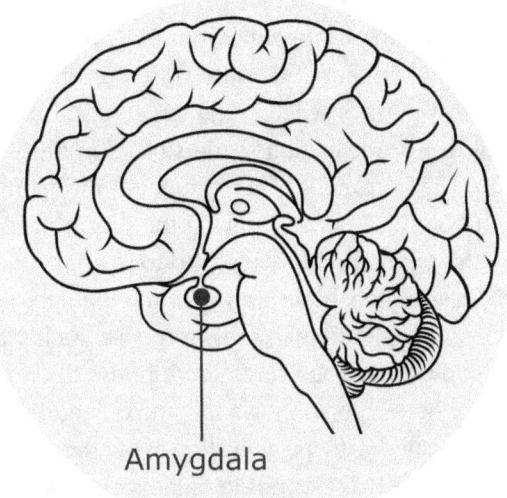

Amygdala

Figure 2.2 Simplified illustration of the human brain showing the location of the amygdala.

When the amygdala detects a potential danger, such as a loud noise (or even a psychological threat like relationship conflict), it initiates the *'fight or flight'* response, a survival mechanism first theorised by physiologist Walter Cannon (1915). You may recognise this phrase from earlier. Essentially, it's your body's automatic response to the amygdala's threat signals, preparing you to confront the danger ('fight') or run far away ('flight'). This response is driven by our sympathetic nervous system, which triggers physiological symptoms like enhanced alertness, increased breathing and heart rate, increased blood sugar and dilated pupils (McCarty, 2016). It also causes the release of stress hormones, such as adrenaline and cortisol, which prepare the body for a more efficient response to danger (Chu et al., 2024). This was used way back when we had to run away from T-Rexs and snakes. It was a means of survival, enabling us to respond to dangerous situations quickly.

So, it turns out my brain isn't trying to ruin my life completely—it's just doing its job to protect me. Sometimes it presses the panic button when it doesn't need to. I guess it helps to know my brain is not against me. We just need to learn how to work together…

Me

Studies have shown that when you vividly imagine a stressful situation, like an upcoming presentation or interview, your body reacts in the same way it does when it actually happens. This is because our brains fire up the same neural pathways regardless of whether the threat posed is real or fabricated, elevating cortisol levels and initiating the stress response (Reddan, Wager & Schiller, 2018). Cannon's work was influential in linking our emotional experiences with bodily responses, paving the way for our modern understanding of how the brain and body respond to stress.

More recently, researchers have proposed that the fight or flight response doesn't fully encapsulate the human stress response. Rather than 'fighting' or 'fleeing', some people 'freeze' or 'fawn' in response to danger. As the word implies, 'freeze' is where a person stays still and quiet until the threat settles. This response is associated with the activation of our parasympathetic nervous system, which is essentially the opposite of the sympathetic nervous system. Our parasympathetic nervous system calms the body down once the danger has passed, slowing down our breathing and heart rate, makes our pupils smaller and lowers blood sugar levels, returning the body to a restful state.

The 'fawn' response is where a person tries to please the attacker, in an attempt to prevent harm (Knight, 2025). Nowadays, the 'fawn' response is often used in the context of trauma theory and recovery, where keeping an abuser happy feels like the safest way to avoid conflict. People who are exposed to environments like this may people-please excessively, apologise often even when they're not in the wrong, prioritise others at the expense of their own wellbeing—all in order to stay emotionally and physically safe. Theorists believe the fawn response involves a mix of the sympathetic (fight or flight) and parasympathetic (freeze) responses, where our body remains 'calm' or 'submissive' on the outside, but on the inside it's anxious and hyperconscious of others' expectations and needs (Owca, 2020).

PRO TIP: Humming to your favourite song can actually ease anxiety. It does this by producing vocal vibrations which stimulate the vagus nerve. This weakens your fight or flight response and calms your nervous system (Trivedi et al., 2023).

Nowadays, the fight or flight response can be initiated in response to stressors that aren't actually life-threatening (I don't see any T-rexes running havoc these days!). In modern life, our amygdala is often overactivated, leading to elevated anxiety which is out of proportion to the real danger posed (Orji & Ita, 2024).

Let's take a look at an example of how the fight or flight response may play out in a real-life context:

Amber's Dilemma: To Fight or Not to Fight

It was a regular Monday evening. Amber was lying in bed, half-watching the latest hot Netflix series while scrolling through her phone (it's funny how we think we can multi-task—when really, we're just scrolling!), when a message pops up in her Uni group chat. One of her friends had sent a passive-aggressive message, calling Amber out for not being supportive when it mattered. Just minutes earlier, the same friend had sent her a direct message asking for help, which she hadn't got around to replying to... Amber froze. She could feel her heart pounding at a million miles an hour. Her stomach felt uncomfortable, and she started panicking. She kept re-reading the message, hoping her eyes were deceiving her. She felt a mix of emotions—sad, angry, confused—and didn't know what to do. How could she be outed like this when she hadn't done anything wrong? And worse—what if everyone else in the group chat believed them? This was Amber's fight-or-flight response in action. Even though there was no physical danger, her brain still interpreted the digital threat as dangerous. It was a threat to her social standing and her safety within her tribe.

She had two options:

- **Fight:** Stand up for herself. Immediately send a defensive message, to prove her side of the story, maybe even lash out.
- **Flight:** Flee as quickly as humanly possible. Confrontation is not for the faint hearted. Leave the group chat, throw her phone in the river Thames, avoid reading any replies, or better still—delete all social media, move to the mountains and become a monk.

Her nervous system was hard at work—adrenaline and cortisol pumping through her body, thoughts racing, breathing quickening. Her brain was in protection mode.

Amber paused, took a few deep breaths, and gave herself some time to re-coup. She responded calmly and the situation was resolved. In the end, she didn't fight or flee. No drama. No explosions. No swift WhatsApp exits.

Amber's experience shows why understanding your own fight-or-flight response is important—it helps you identify when your brain has hit the alarm and gives you the chance to pause and plan your next step with clarity.

2.1 No Amygdala, No Problem? Think Again

Research on animals shows those without an amygdala don't respond to fear appropriately. This is a major problem for our furry friends as they are less likely to be able to protect themselves against predators. Think of any David Attenborough documentary you've watched. Most of them feature a cute innocent animal going about their business with a predator lurking in the distance, ready to pounce on their dinner. If the little cutie doesn't have the appropriate threat detection signals, they can forget about their evening plans as they aren't likely to make it past breakfast.

Many studies have looked at rats (and other rodents). This is for several reasons which I'll briefly outline. Firstly, their brain structure is similar in many key ways to that of humans, e.g. they have an amygdala, which makes them a good comparison model for brain research (Clark & Squire, 2013). Additionally, it has been viewed as *more* ethical to study rats than humans (Shapiro, 1998). Don't come at me for saying that—this is a highly contentious opinion, not my own. Regardless of personal views, studies on rats have provided rich insights into brain function and emotional processing from vast amounts of lesion studies (where a particular brain area is removed or damaged) to directly observe cause-and-effect relationships. Let's look at a specific example.

Tiny Brains, Big Insights

One study investigated the response of rats, who had lesions in their amygdala, to cats. Normal rats typically show strong fear responses to their predators, such as avoiding or freezing. However, the rats with lesions did not show this behaviour. In some cases, they actually strolled on over to the cats without a care in the world. Bold move! Let's just say… they regretted their laid-back attitude pretty quickly! (Blanchard & Blanchard, 1972)

To make this all a bit more relatable, let's take a look at a real-life example from a human.

The Woman with No Fear

If you've studied psychology, you'll know about the infamous SM (or you haven't been listening!). She was diagnosed with Urbach-Wiethe disease, a rare genetic disorder which alters the brain and body, which resulted in damage to her amygdala. Researchers were shocked to find that she didn't experience fear, even when exposed to dangerous snakes or approaching a haunted house. In both cases, she didn't experience the usual bodily reactions, like increased heart rate or avoidance behaviour. In fact, she showed little to no physiological response at all! She was essentially fearless... a real-life fear-free superhero! While that might seem cool, it actually posed a serious danger for her survival. Think about it, she would interact with the dangerous snake without understanding it could harm or kill her. Despite her impaired fear processing, she did experience other emotions, such as happiness and sadness, and showed normal cognitive functioning, i.e. she could understand fear in others but couldn't experience it herself. This case was huge in the world of psychology and neuroscience. It showcased just how important the amygdala is in our emotional processing and our ability to detect threats. (Tranel et al., 2006)

These examples demonstrate the importance and influence of the amygdala for both humans and animals when it comes to threat responses. However, sometimes it can become overactive, causing our brain to detect a threat when there isn't one. But fear not, my friends—there is hope! There are various ways to manage these responses, which we'll come to later.

PRO TIP: If you gently tap your opposite shoulders or knees in a right-left rhythm for a couple minutes, you are engaging in what is called 'bilateral stimulation'. It is a technique used to calm the nervous system and regulate emotions by reducing amygdala activity (Pagani et al., 2017).

Reflect & Act: High Alert

Reflect:
- Can you recall a time when your body went into 'fight or flight' mode? How did your body react? Was it a real danger or false alarm?

Act:
- Everyone's stress signals are different. Start to recognise what yours are (e.g. racing heart rate, sweating). To help you, we'll look at some short breathing exercises in a later chapter.

Key Takeaways

Before we move on, here's what to remember from this chapter:

- The amygdala may be small, but it is an incredibly powerful part of the brain, helping us detect threats and initiate the body's fear response.
- It plays a crucial role in the 'fight or flight' response—activated when we sense real or perceived danger.
- An overactive amygdala can lead to physical symptoms like an elevated breathing and heart rate.
- Studies show the importance of the amygdala in fear processing—rodent studies where amygdala lesions reduced fear, and the famous case of SM.

Mission accomplished: You've Got the Brain Scoop

Next stop: The inner workings of your fear response? Light work. So… what causes anxiety to go off in the first place? Let's break down the theories behind anxiety.

References

Blanchard, R. J. & Blanchard, D. C. (1972). Effects of hippocampal lesions on the rat's reaction to a cat. *Journal of comparative and physiological psychology*, 78(1), 77.

Cannon, W. B. (1915). *Bodily changes in pain, hunger, fear and rage: An account of recent researches into the function of emotional excitement*. D. Appleton. https://doi.org/10.1037/10013-000.

Chu, B., Marwaha, K., Sanvictores, T., Awosika, A. O. & Ayers, D. (2024). Physiology, stress reaction. In *StatPearls [Internet]*. StatPearls Publishing. https://www.ncbi.nlm.nih.gov/books/NBK541120/.

Clark, R. E. & Squire, L. R. (2013). Similarity in form and function of the hippocampus in rodents, monkeys, and humans. *Proceedings of the National Academy of Sciences*, 110 (supplement 2), 10365–10370.

Knight, J. D. (2025). Is the nervous system sympathetic? *Journal of Surgery and Medical Case Reports*, 2(2), 1–4.

Lent, R., Azevedo, F. A., Andrade-Moraes, C. H. & Pinto, A. V. (2012). How many neurons do you have? Some dogmas of quantitative neuroscience under revision. *European Journal of Neuroscience*, 35(1), 1–9.

Linsambarth, S., Moraga-Amaro, R., Quintana-Donoso, D., Rojas, S. & Stehberg, J. (2017). The amygdala and anxiety. In B. Ferry (Ed.), *The amygdala: Where emotions shape perception, learning and memories*. InTechOpen, 139–171. https://doi.org/10.5772/intechopen.68618.

McCarty, R. (2016). The fight-or-flight response: A cornerstone of stress research. In G. Fink (Ed.), *Stress: Concepts, cognition, emotion, and behavior* (pp. 33–37). Academic Press. https://doi.org/10.1016/B978-0-12-800951-2.00004-2.

Orji, L. C. & Ita, U. A. (2024). Amygdala hijack: Contemporary insights into causes, correlates and consequences. *Midwifery*, 7(3), 102–111.

Owca, J. (2020). *The association between a psychotherapist's theoretical orientation and perception of complex trauma and repressed anger in the fawn response* (PhD diss., The Chicago School of Professional Psychology).

Pagani, M., Di Lorenzo, G., Monaco, L., Daverio, A., Giannoudas, I., La Porta, P., Verardo, A. R., Niolu, C, Fernandez, I. & Siracusano, A. (2015). Neurobiological response to EMDR therapy in clients with different psychological traumas. *Frontiers in Psychology*, 6, 1614.

Reddan, M. C., Wager, T. D. & Schiller, D. (2018). Attenuating neural threat expression with imagination. *Neuron*, 100(4), 994–1005.

Shapiro, K. J. (1998). *Animal models of human psychology: Critique of science, ethics, and policy*. Seattle: Hogrefe & Huber.

Tranel, D., Gullickson, G., Koch, M. & Adolphs, R. (2006). Altered experience of emotion following bilateral amygdala damage. *Cognitive neuropsychiatry*, 11(3), 219–232.

Trivedi, G., Sharma, K., Saboo, B., Kathirvel, S., Konat, A., Zapadia, V., Prajapati, P. J., Benani, U., Patel, K. & Shah, S. (2023). Humming (simple Bhramari Pranayama) as a stress buster: A holter-based study to analyze heart rate variability (HRV) parameters during Bhramari, physical activity, emotional stress, and sleep. *Cureus*, 15(4), e37527.

3 The Anxiety Time Machine

Uncovering the Secrets of Stress

There's a science to the stuff in my head → that's comforting weirdly!

Figure 3.1 A glimpse into my thoughts: a page from my personal journal.

The greatest weapon against stress is our ability to choose one thought over another.

William James, known as the 'Father of American Psychology'

> **GOAL:** To break down three major explanations for anxiety, so you can see anxiety from different lenses and better understand your experience.

3.1 Psych-101 (But Make It Make Sense)

When you hear the word 'theory', you probably think you're about to be bombarded with scientific, technical jargon reserved for only the elite bookworms amongst us. Well, I'm here to tell you that it's not, in fact, that intimidating. It's basically just a set of ideas or principles which aim to explain a particular *thing* that is testable (Gorelick, 2011). I'm informing you of this fun fact because it is relevant for understanding anxiety and will make this chapter

DOI: 10.4324/9781003670117-4

more digestible. In the world of anxiety, there are different theories to explain human behaviour. Scientists can test these different theories through research, which is constantly progressing year on year. As our understanding of psychological phenomena changes, theories need to be adapted to fit in with an ever-changing landscape. I'm not going to attempt to explain all theories of anxiety as this is not necessary nor is it useful. I will, however, briefly outline a few of the major psychological theories, to provide a basic level of under-standing of why we behave the way we do, as well as give context for many of the psychological treatments routinely administered today.

You won't believe it but some people way back when actually spent their lives trying to understand why we think and feel the way we do. There's a science to the stuff in my head… that's comforting at least.

Me

3.2 How Do Hidden Thoughts Shape Your Feelings?

The psychodynamic theory was one of the first to be introduced and may seem a little far-fetched to some of you (and rightly so!). Sigmund Freud, coined the 'Founder of Psychoanalysis', proposed that our childhood expe-riences play a vital role in determining our behaviour later in life (true!), but some of his concepts are, shall we say, outside the box (Traylor et al., 2022). Take the Oedipus complex, a part of his theory on psychosexual development (Lebovici, 1982). The name 'Oedipus' is a character in Greek mythology who kills his father and marries his mother. You're intrigued now, aren't you! Freud believed that around the age of three, young boys experience an unconscious desire for their mother and see their father as their rival for her affection. The 'Electra' complex is the opposite, where young girls experience an unconscious desire for their father and rivalry with their mother (Khan & Haider, 2015). You now get what I mean by 'out-side the box'!

In essence, the psychodynamic theory sought to understand the source of unconscious behaviour. Freud believed that the mind has three parts (conscious, unconscious and preconscious) and that much of the mind lay beneath consciousness.

Freud suggested that our personality is made up of three parts: the id, the ego and the superego (Rennison, 2015). Each of these allows us access into the 'why' behind human behaviour. Let's break them down:

ID: the part of the mind which seeks immediate gratification for our urges (a.k.a. 'pleasure seeker')

SUPEREGO: the moral component of the mind, embodying societal standards (a.k.a. 'conscience')

EGO: the realistic part of mind which acts as a mediator between the urges of the id and the morals of the superego.

The id operates unconsciously whilst the ego and superego can operate either consciously or unconsciously. Many people use the iceberg analogy to make it a little easier to understand. See Figure 3.2.

Freud's theory of anxiety has evolved over time. Initially he proposed that the id, ego and superego can come into conflict with one another. If the ego

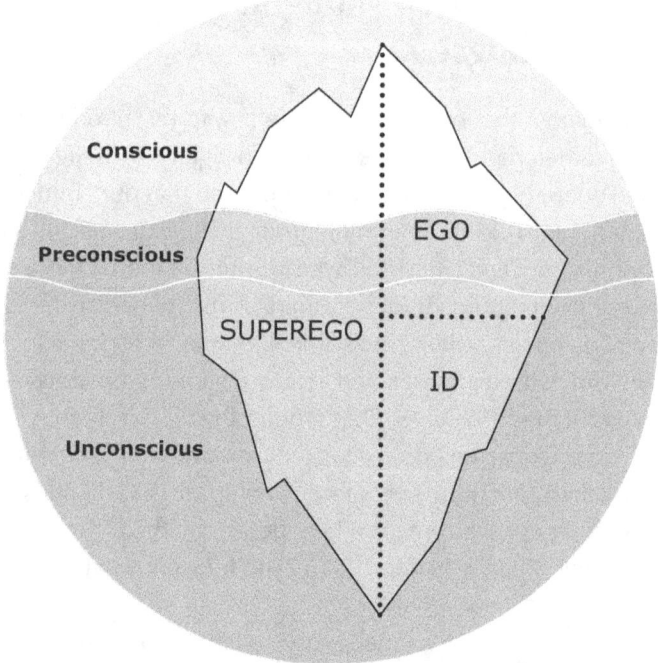

Figure 3.2 Freud's iceberg analogy of the mind, illustrating the id, ego and superego in relation to the conscious, preconscious and unconscious.

(a.k.a. the mediator) is unable to resolve conflict between the id and super-ego, this may precipitate anxiety. Freud described the ego as *'the actual seat of anxiety'*, emphasising the impact of internal conflict.

Researchers have found various psychological issues, including higher levels of anxiety, in adults who were punished for expressing id impulses in childhood.

- **Mills and Rubin (1990)** found that children who were harshly disciplined had higher levels of anxiety and depression in adolescence*.
- **McLeod, Wood and Weisz (2007)** assessed the effects of parenting practices on later adulthood. They found that harsh parenting was strongly associated with the development of anxiety disorders.

It is important to note that I am not implying that discipline is a bad thing. On the contrary, young people need boundaries (as do many old people, but that's for a different book…). Without such, the world would be feral! However, there is a fine line between discipline that teaches appropriate boundaries and discipline that's overly harsh and restrictive.

Let's make it more relatable:

Blame It on the Superego

Imagine someone who constantly second-guesses themselves—even over small choices like what to wear. They feel overwhelming pressure to make the 'right' decision and worry about being judged if they don't. The psychodynamic theory would suggest that this pattern may stem from overly strict or critical parenting in childhood, where even the slightest flaws were reprimanded. This can lead to the development of an overly critical superego—the part of the mind that acts like an internalised voice of morality and authority, constantly enforcing rules and handing out guilt for anything short of perfection. The superego is working over-time, punishing them with guilt or anxiety when they do. So, even later in life, a rather trivial decision may in fact feel suffocating to many people—with their inner critic ready and raring to pounce when they trip.

Many people question Freud's explanations of psychological phenomena; needless to say, I can understand why! However, agree or not with his ideas, Freud remains a significant figure and pioneer in the world of psychology, not least for being the first to place value on the effect of childhood experiences on behaviour in adulthood.

3.3 Where Does My Anxious Behaviour Come From?

This one might seem slightly more realistic (sorry, Freud!). Behavioural theorists suggest that anxiety and phobias are the result of conditioning, which is a learning process where behaviours are attained or altered through interactions with the environment (Davey, 2017). John B. Watson (a behaviourist) believed that anxiety can be developed. Something that is initially 'neutral' can elicit a fearful response after undergoing what is known as 'classical conditioning'.

I'm going to run you through a famous psychological case of classical conditioning in action. This one may be familiar to some of you psychology whizzes out there—*Pavlov's Dogs*—an investigation in the digestion of dogs (Adams, 2020). See Figure 3.3.

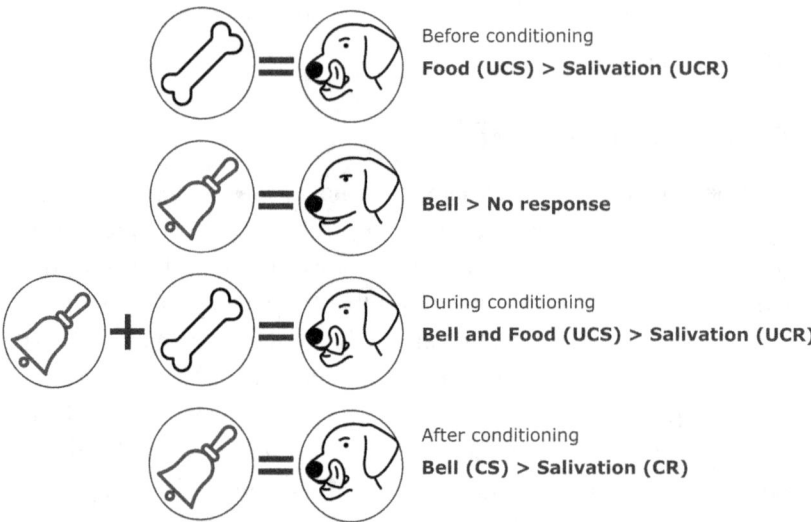

Before conditioning
Food (UCS) > Salivation (UCR)

Bell > No response

During conditioning
Bell and Food (UCS) > Salivation (UCR)

After conditioning
Bell (CS) > Salivation (CR)

Figure 3.3 Pavlov's classical conditioning: a neutral stimulus paired with food leads to a learned salivation response.

- A lab assistant regularly attended the lab to give some dogs their food.
- After some time, Pavlov (an experimenter) realised that the dogs salivated in the presence of the lab assistant, even before any food was shown to them. They had *associated* food with the lab assistant.

- This intrigued him and he decided to investigate further.
- He paired a 'neutral' stimulus—a bell—with food. Over time, the dogs had learned that the sound of the bell ringing meant food was coming and thus associated the bell with food and salivated.
- After several repetitions, the dogs salivated at the sound of the bell, even when no food was presented.
- Pavlov concluded that the dogs had been conditioned to associate the bell with food.

So why is this relevant to anxiety, you ask? Well, good question! We can understand anxiety in humans through classical conditioning. For example, an individual may associate a non-threatening, 'neutral' stimulus (like a bell) with a negative experience, turning it into something they fear. Over time, this fear may generalise to other similar situations. It's easier to explain this point with a real-life example.

From Car Crash to Cold Sweat

Meet Max, who was involved in a car accident last year. The accident itself is the unconditioned stimulus, and the anxiety Max felt during the accident is the unconditioned response. Over time, signals associated with the accident—such as the sound of the car crashing—may become the conditioned stimuli. As a result, when Max hears these sounds it may trigger his anxiety, even when there is no actual threat, because the sounds have become associated with the initial traumatic experience.

Phobias can be viewed through a similar lens of classical conditioning, as they often develop when a neutral stimulus becomes associated with fear or anxiety.

1. Imagine a person gets bitten by a dog. The bite, the unconditioned stimulus, leads to fear, the unconditioned response. As time goes on, when the person sees a dog (conditioned stimulus), they experience anxiety (conditioned response).
2. Many people experience anxiety about needles (forgive me for reminding you of the COVID pandemic!). Just one 'bad' experience with a needle can cause a lifelong fear. Imagine you went for your COVID vaccination

(unconditioned stimulus) and the pain caused you to wince and cry (unconditioned response). You may then associate the needle (conditioned stimulus) with pain. Consequently, the sight of needles in the future makes you cry (conditioned response).

3. Imagine you experience a painful medical procedure in the hospital (unconditioned stimulus) which is very traumatic (unconditioned response). You then begin to associate the hospital (conditioned stimulus) with distress and unease. Future visits to the hospital cause you to feel anxious and fearful (conditioned response).

3.4 What Role Do Thoughts Play in My Anxiety?

Cognitive-Behavioural Theory (CBT) is a widely used approach for navigating the complex interplay of mental processes that drive many mental health problems, including anxiety (Garland & Thyer, 2012). You may have heard of cognitive-behavioural therapy, a talking therapy that's widely administered across the national healthcare system to help treat various mental health problems. Think of CBT as an extension of behavioural theory, bringing our thought processes, feelings and behaviour together.

A situation can be broken down into four aspects: **thoughts, emotions, physical sensations and behaviours**. These are interlinked, i.e. our thoughts influence our emotions, physical sensations and behaviours, whilst our behaviours can reinforce our thoughts, physical sensations and emotions. The complex interplay of these mechanisms forms a 'feedback loop', a central term in many psychological theories (such as Cognitive Behaviour Therapy). Imagine a continuous loop where the output of a process influences its own input. Understanding and intervening in these feedback loops can promote better mental and physical wellbeing.

Singer Adele has openly shared her struggles with performance anxiety, describing an overwhelming fear of audiences. On one occasion, it was so bad she fled a show through a fire exit. Another time, she was physically ill before going on stage. Despite how successful she is, she's shared how frequently she experiences anxiety attacks, making touring really challenging.

For example:

1. **What's going on in my head:** You might catch yourself thinking, *'Something bad is about to happen.'*
2. **What it makes me feel:** That thought can make you feel anxious, nervous or even overwhelmed. You might notice your heart racing, your breathing getting quicker, or you're having difficulty concentrating.
3. **What I do about it:** Naturally, you'll want to run away from whatever's making you feel this way, like avoiding the situation entirely. But doing this only makes the original thought, *'Something bad is going to happen'*, feel even more true. (More on why avoidance isn't always the answer later!)

In the world of psychology, this cycle is referred to as the 'hot-cross bun'. See Figure 3.4.

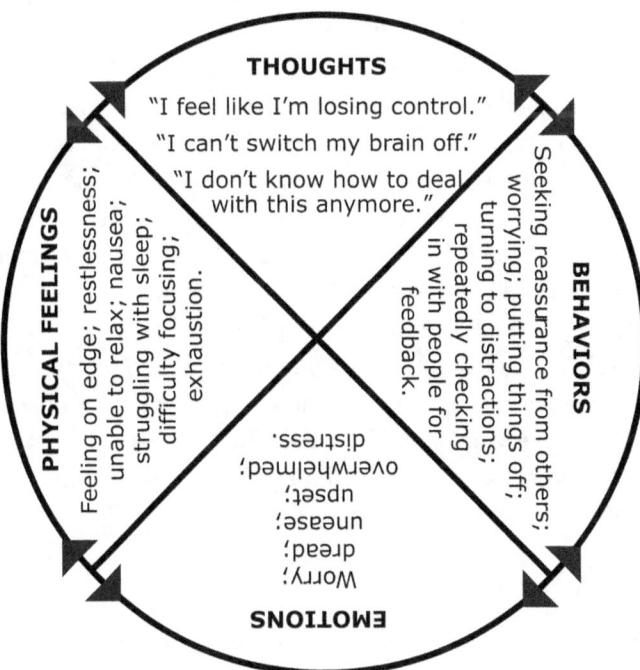

Figure 3.4 The classic CBT Hot Cross Bun analogy brought to life—illustrating how thoughts, emotions, behaviours and physical feelings are all connected.

Let's break it down with an example to make it clearer.

> Tom is 21 and struggles with social anxiety. He often avoids social situations because he fears being judged or embarrassing himself. When he's faced with these situations, his anxiety spikes—his heart races, his stomach goes into knots and his palms become sweaty. These intense feelings and thoughts lead Tom to cancel plans or leave events early, just to escape the discomfort. But by doing this, he only feeds the vicious cycle of social anxiety, making it harder for him to break free.

In Tom's case:

- **Thoughts:** 'They will judge me', 'I will embarrass myself'
- **Emotions:** Fear, anxiety
- **Physical sensations:** Racing heart, stomach cramps, sweating
- **Behaviour:** Cancels plans, leaves early

Tom's experience shows how the cycle of negative thoughts, feelings and behaviours can reinforce anxiety, making it harder to break out of. Winston Churchill, former Prime Minister, famously once said, *'I remember the story of the old man who said on his deathbed that he had had a lot of trouble in his life, most of which had never happened'*—a powerful reminder that many of our worries in life exist solely in our imagination.

Cognitive-behavioural therapy aims to interrupt this cycle by helping people identify and challenge their unhelpful thoughts and behaviours through learning new ways to cope, shift mindset, and gradually face situations without feeling overwhelmed. You might be wondering what cognitive-behavioural therapy looks like in real life, so here's an example of how I've tried to apply some of the principles of CBT in my own life.

From Panic to Perspective

When I get anxious about something, such as missing a flight, I try to pause and ask myself: *What's the worst that could actually happen?* In this case, the worst is… I miss the flight. Is that annoying? Hell yes! Is it fatal? Definitely not. It might throw off my plans, cost me time or money, and cause me to go a bit psychotic, but in the grand scheme of things, it's not going to ruin my life. This kind of thinking helps me gain some perspective. I try to use this logic in other areas of life too. It doesn't make the anxiety automatically vanish, but it takes the edge off – and sometimes, that's all you need.

Reflect & Act: Mindset Switcheroo

Reflect:
- Think of a recent moment you felt anxious. What was your main thought? How did it make you feel? What did you do?

Act:
- Challenge it! Is there any concrete evidence to support it? Can you rephrase it in a more helpful and compassionate way? How does this new version make you feel?

Supplement your experience via the worksheet in Appendix A of the Additional Resources.

Key Takeaways

Before we move on, here's what to remember from this chapter:

- Psychodynamic, behavioural and cognitive theories are three big psychological theories that help explain anxiety.
- Psychodynamic theory explores how anxiety can arise from inner conflict and past experiences.
- Behavioural theorists view anxiety as a learned response through conditioning—a neutral stimulus becomes associated with fear or anxiety.
- Cognitive Behavioural Theory (CBT) focuses on how our thoughts, feelings and behaviours interact. We can change unhelpful thought patterns to help reduce anxiety.

Mission accomplished: Mind Hacked (Three Ways!)

Next stop: Now that you've got the lowdown on what drives our behaviour, it's time to explore how anxiety shows up in the mind and body—what you might think, feel and experience when it takes hold.

References

Adams, M. (2020). The kingdom of dogs: Understanding Pavlov's experiments as human–animal relationships. *Theory & Psychology, 30*(1), 121–141.

Davey, G. (2017). Conditioning principles, behaviourism and behaviour therapy. In *Applications of conditioning theory* (pp. 189–214). Routledge.

Garland, E. L. & Thyer, B. A. (2012). Cognitive-behavioural approach. In M. Gray & S. A. Webb (Eds.), *Social work theories and methods* (pp. 159–174). SAGE Publications.

Gorelick, R. (2011). What is theory? *Ideas in Ecology and Evolution, 4*(1), 1–10.

Khan, M. & Haider, K. (2015). Girls' first love; their fathers: Freudian theory Electra complex. *Research Journal of Language, Literature and Humanities, 2*(11), 1–4.

Lebovici, S. (1982). The origins and development of the Oedipus complex. *The International Journal of Psycho-Analysis, 63*, 201.

McLeod, B. D., Wood, J. J. & Weisz, J. R. (2007). Examining the association between parenting and childhood anxiety: A meta-analysis. *Clinical Psychology Review, 27*(2), 155–172.

Mills, R. S. & Rubin, K. H. (1990). Parental beliefs about problematic social behaviors in early childhood. *Child Development, 61*(1), 138–151.

Rennison, N. (2015). *Freud and psychoanalysis: Everything you need to know about id, ego, super-ego and more.* Oldcastle Books.

Traylor, J., Overstreet, L. & Lang, D. (2022). Psychodynamic theory: Freud. In D. Lang (Ed.), *Individual and family development, health, and well-being.* Iowa State University Digital Press. https://iastate.pressbooks.pub/individual familydevelopment/chapter/freuds-psychodynamic-theory/.

4 | Inside Anxiety
Sweaty Palms and Racing Thoughts

Anxiety isn't just thoughts.
It's physical too. It's ALL connected.
It's REAL.

Figure 4.1 A glimpse into my thoughts: a page from my personal journal.

It's not about controlling your thoughts, but about learning not to let them control you.

Anonymous

> **GOAL:** To help you understand how anxiety may affect your psychological state and physical body, so you can recognise the symptoms and better manage them.

Archie's Anxiety Avalanche

Archie wakes up to an uncomfortable knot in his stomach, his mind racing with unwanted thoughts—*'What if I can't get my words out in the team meeting?' 'What if forget my script?'* He drags himself out of bed to get ready, his heart and breathing quickening by the minute. As he puts on his suit tie, he notices beads of sweat forming on his palms, and then suddenly appearing on his forehead. He wipes his face with his hand, hoping it will clear it from sight, but it comes back

DOI: 10.4324/9781003670117-5

moments later. His muscles begin to tense so he takes a long, laborious stretch of his upper body, hoping this will relax him. No luck, so he battles on with the morning, despite it feeling like he's already done two days back-to-back without sleep.

Throughout the day, Archie has difficulty focusing. Minor noise feels exaggerated, and he's easily startled. His stomach does somersaults in a less-than-ideal manner, sometimes causing him to feel nauseous. He fidgets constantly, tapping his foot so fast, you'd think he was about to unlock a new level in Guitar Hero. So much pent-up energy and no place for it to go.

By the time he gets home from the office that evening, he is totally fried, but will he be able to sleep tonight? No chance with his racing mind. He replays the day's worries like a new favourite song you play on repeat—to death. Physically tapped out and mentally drained, Archie lies awake, caught in the anxiety chokehold.

Archie's experience gives us an insight into how anxiety affects both the mind and the body. It shows up in our thoughts and physical sensations when we least expect it, and in ways we can't predict. It's annoying, right?

In the section below, we'll explore the multiple ways anxiety can greet you. It may trigger a trip down memory lane, reminding you of times when anxiety may have cropped up to say hello without you actually realising it was anxiety. That's how sneaky is it! We'll break down the most common psychological and physical symptoms that people experience. Getting familiar with these is the first step towards understanding anxiety in yourself or others—and finding ways to outsmart it. You might have experienced every single one of the below, definitely a few, and almost certainly one.

It's bizarre how I can be anxious about something and next thing you know my whole body wants to get involved... it feels as though my heart is going to jump out of my chest and oh the clammy hands! For so long I was confused. Embarrassed. Now I know anxiety isn't just thoughts—it's physical too. It's all connected. It's REAL...

Me

4.1 How Does Anxiety Impact My Mind?

- **Restlessness:** You may find it hard to sit still and unwind, as if your mind wants to be constantly doing something and won't turn off. You may notice you fidget a lot, or when you're finally settling down, you suddenly get the urge to get up to do something—even when there's no real need. As if life isn't exhausting enough!
- **Panic:** You may experience sudden feelings of fear or panic that seem to come out of the blue, making small and insignificant activities feel completely overwhelming. This may seem like an alarm has suddenly gone off, and all you want to do is escape, even if you're not sure why.
- **Trouble focusing:** You may have difficulty concentrating on simple tasks as you're preoccupied with anxious thoughts. Your mind may drift off whilst you're trying to complete a task at work, causing it to take triple the time it should. Do you recall a time when you had to read a sentence five times for it to actually sink in? Well, this happens to me more regularly than I like to admit! Wouldn't it be nice if our brain cooperated and did what we asked for at least half the working week? Sometimes it feels as though it's taken an unexpected annual leave!
- **Irritability:** You may feel as though you get frustrated more easily over small things, causing you to snap or get in a funk! Minor inconveniences feel catastrophic—like when Kim Kardashian lost her diamond earring in the ocean whilst on vacation in Bora Bora... now that's not for the faint-hearted!
- **Overwhelmed:** You may feel like everything is piling up and you just want to scream. Simple tasks are too much to take on with the little energy you have to spare, and you feel like you're drowning. Your mind is in chaos—much like an episode of Dirty House Rescue: Queens of Clean, where the sheer volume of clutter makes it hard to know where to begin!

Simone Biles, American gymnast, has expressed how important it is to prioritise mental health in sport. She shared how she took some time out to take proper care of herself and tune in to how she was feeling, both physically and emotionally. This is a powerful reminder that we need to listen what our body is telling us. Sometimes, you need to take a small step back to take a big one forward.

4.2 How Does Anxiety Affect My Body?

- **Sweating:** You may notice yourself sweating excessively, even when you're not exerting yourself at all. It may start with the palms of your hands, and spread to different areas of your body, like your forehead, upper lip (often referred to as a 'SULA'- sweaty upper lip alert!) or your underarms. As a self-professed sweaty girl, I've found this symptom of anxiety especially difficult. You can visibly see when someone is sweating, which triggers embarrassment and, great, even more sweat!

- **Increased heart rate:** You may notice your heart beating faster than normal, like it's finally decided to run that marathon you've had in the diary for the past year but never quite got round to doing. Only you're not running, nor are you walking, so why does it feel like it's about to jump out of your chest? This may also come as surprise and so make you feel more out of breath and on edge.

- **Fatigue:** Given the above, it's unsurprising that anxiety can be totally exhausting. When your mind is on overdrive, it uses up a significant amount of energy, leaving you feeling drained, even after a long night's sleep. This creates a vicious cycle where fatigue worsens your anxiety, and anxiety worsens your fatigue.

- **Sleep issues:** Anxiety can cause trouble getting to sleep, as your mind is preoccupied with anxious thoughts. You may lie awake for hours despite feeling exhausted, and/or wake up frequently during the night and struggle to get back to sleep. You get up in the morning never feeling well rested, which heightens your anxiety and makes it increasingly difficult to break the repeating loop of sleep deprivation and anxiety (fear not—we'll explore some top tips to improve your sleep in a later chapter).

- **Gastrointestinal issues:** Anxiety can affect the body's fight or flight response, disrupting digestion and causing problems like nausea, diarrhoea, constipation and stomach pains. It might feel like your stomach is in knots (sit tight—more on this later).

- **Disturbed eating habits:** You may notice a change in your appetite. Occasionally anxiety can lead to a loss of interest in food, where you forget to eat or don't find any enjoyment when you do. Other times, it causes you to turn to food for comfort, which in some cases can lead to overeating. Either way, the outcome is usually tiredness and frustration, which can make managing your anxiety even more tricky!

Let's dig a little deeper. Take the example of an exam, a situation which all of us are bound to encounter at some stage in our life (maybe not if you were a COVID-era baby, but stick with me!). In the days or hours leading up to the exam, you may experience nausea, vomiting, constipation and/or diarrhoea. This is a totally normal result of anxiety. These feelings may put you off your food. On the flip side, some individuals use food as a form of comfort, reaching for the chocolate bar to ease their uneasiness. This may lead to overconsumption when their body doesn't really need it. Simply knowing that worry/stress/anxiety can influence your appetite can go a long way in helping you navigate your nerves during exam periods and in other anxiety-provoking scenarios.

- **Avoidance:** You may avoid certain people, places or situations which cause you to feel uneasy. This is a very common symptom of people who experience anxiety and can worsen it dramatically (Mahoney et al., 2016). Anxiety warns us to avoid situations that cause us discomfort. This is essentially a quick fix, getting you out of a scary situation, but it leads to prolonged difficulties. It teaches your brain that you need to keep running to feel safe! This is how the anxiety feedback loop traps you.

PRO TIP: One solution to get through this is exposure—gradually facing the thing that makes you anxious. Scary (and I hear you), but there's a reason why it's one of the most effective treatments for helping people overcome fears and anxiety disorders. Take a fear of public speaking—doing it as much as possible can help your brain learn that it isn't as scary as it feels. Over time, it'll become easier and less terrifying, until it falls comfortably within your comfort zone.

Let's take a look at a real-life example. My mum once shared a story about her experience with a spider named Erica (bear with me on this one!):

Erica the Spider

My mum had been plagued by a crippling fear of spiders since a young age, but one day, everything changed. She was in her mid-20s working on a film set that featured a tarantula (don't ask me why—some things are better left unexplained!). At first, my mum was really scared about being in the same vicinity as this eight-legged creature, taking as many opportunities as possible to go for a break to avoid eye contact with it. But, as if by some miracle, as the hours passed, she become less and less worried about Erica's every move. By the end of the shoot, after seeing how calm the handler was with Erica, mum put on her big girl boots and decided to give it a go herself. (Go Mum!) From starting the day petrified of being in the same room as Erica, she was now stood there holding the fluff ball in her hands. She was so proud of herself! Whilst she's not intending on starting a spider fan club anytime soon, she no longer breaks into a cold sweat at the sight of one.

That said, if you feel your anxiety has become overwhelming to the point where public speaking feels totally impossible, know this: your struggle is valid. You're not alone and it's okay to need some support. Reaching out can help you navigate these challenges and find effective ways to manage them whilst building confidence in a way that feels safe and sustainable.

Avoidance is the best short-term strategy to escape conflict, and the best long-term strategy to ensure suffering.
Brendon Burchard, author and high-performance coach

Reflect & Act: Get to Know Yourself!

Reflect:
• Can you identify two mind or body symptoms you notice when you feel anxious? For example, do you experience muscle tension, or perhaps difficulty concentrating?

Act:
• Close your eyes and try focusing on your heartbeat for a minute. Just notice your sensations without trying to fix them.

Key Takeaways

Before we move on, here's what to remember from this chapter:

• Anxiety impacts both the mind and body.
• Psychological symptoms may include racing thoughts, difficulty concentrating and overwhelm.

- Physical symptoms such as increased heartrate, sweating and sleep issues are also common.
- Recognising the signs is the first step to managing anxiety effectively and taking back control.

Mission accomplished: Exploring Anxiety's Mind and Body Effects

Next stop: Now you've gained a solid understanding of how anxiety manifests in the mind and body, let's explore how anxiety specifically shows up for young adults in this stage of life, and how the current climate and challenges play a role in shaping these experiences.

Reference

Mahoney, A. E., Hobbs, M. J., Newby, J. M., Williams, A. D., Sunderland, M. & Andrews, G. (2016). The Worry Behaviors Inventory: Assessing the behavioral avoidance associated with generalized anxiety disorder. *Journal of Affective Disorders, 203*, 256–264.

Why Me, Why Now?
Surviving Young Adulthood

Puberty. You are NOT my friend.

Figure 5.1 A glimpse into my thoughts: a page from my personal journal.

Life itself is the most wonderful fairy tale.
Hans Christian Andersen, author

> **GOAL:** To uncover how brain development in young people influences their emotional world and how they handle stress.

Adolescence is a time of big change. I don't know about you, but puberty was a bit of a ball-ache. One moment I was happy, the next angry and then, suddenly, I was blubbing like a toddler who'd just dropped their ice cream! I thought I was going crazy, but it was just the beautiful chaos of puberty working its magic. Puberty causes changes in our body, brain and hormones. The magnitude of these changes depends on individual factors, like age and personal experiences. This is all pretty overwhelming—after all, we're just trying to survive the never-ending battle of figuring out who we really are (no biggy!), but our bodies have *other* plans. It's no surprise we are susceptible to several mental health issues during this time. But fear not, my friends, this is part of growing up and it's usually only temporary—most of the time, teens go on to become fully functioning, healthy adults! The changes that occur are in fact beneficial to healthy development and long-term resilience. So, buckle up and enjoy the ride—this

DOI: 10.4324/9781003670117-6

time, with slightly more insight! Let's dive into the changes that come with entering young adulthood, so we can be prepared to handle them head on.

5.1 Wired for Drama (What Happens Neurologically)

Tennis player Serena Williams (a.k.a. The Queen of the Court) has openly shared her experience growing up. During puberty, she faced many uncomfortable changes to her body and didn't feel that she fitted the usual mould. This led to feelings of anxiety, but over time she learned to accept and love who she was.

The Brain's Growth Spurt

Adolescence is a very important time for our brains. Throughout our teens, the brain is growing in size. Think of it like building a house. You have the foundations, and you're adding new rooms (neural connections) and renovating old ones (what is known as 'pruning'). Some areas take longer to complete than others, but gradually the whole system is growing stronger and more complex (Raising Children Network, 2024). The prefrontal cortex, the part of our brain responsible for decision-making and planning, is the last to fully develop; like the roof, it's the last piece to go on, but the house wouldn't be complete without it. This final piece of the puzzle tends to finish developing in our mid-20s (Simpson, 2016).

Flying off the Handle

The amygdala plays a crucial role in emotional reactions and decision-making (see Chapter 2). When our brain is under construction, our amygdala is more hyperactive than it is when we are children or adults (Tottenham & Galván, 2016). One study showed that the amygdala of adolescents is more active in response to a range of emotions (e.g. happy, fearful, calm) compared with that of children and adults (Hare et al., 2008). Why is this important? Well, when the amygdala—the brain's emotional processing centre—is particularly active, our ability to regulate our emotions appropriately becomes compromised. We are more sensitive to emotional stimuli; thus, we may respond with more anger or anxiety. Think back to a time when you flew off

41

the handle in your teens… we've all been there. Teenhood is undoubtedly an emotional rollercoaster!!

> *Puberty. You are not my friend. One minute I'm fine, the next you've got me screaming or crying without reason. Grrr. It appears that my brain's still building itself. My hormones are partying like they're at a rave in Ibiza. And everyone around me is just SO confused, even if they're trying to hide it. It's a lot… but I'll get through it…*
>
> Me

The Hormonal Tsunami

Our hormonal levels rise throughout adolescence, explaining the mood swings and emotional volatility. The developing brain spills out adrenal stress hormones, sex hormones and growth hormones (Mousikou et al., 2023), such as oestrogen, cortisol and testosterone (we'll revisit these later!). So, what's this all got to do with anxiety, I hear you say? Well, hormones like cortisol are often more reactive during adolescence, which may cause a rise in anxiety (Garcia & O'Neil, 2021). Couple this with our developing brain and, well, we've got an uninvited guest—anxiety, if you hadn't figured—making itself comfortable!

Brain Boost

Testosterone production increases 10 times in adolescent boys.

The Snooze Saga

When we hit adolescence, our 'body's circadian rhythm' (a.k.a. our internal body clock, telling you when to feel awake and sleep) shifts forward by approximately two hours. You can blame this on the sleep hormone 'melatonin', which is released later when we are in our teens compared to when we were younger (about 10–11pm as opposed to 8–9pm; Hersh et al., 2015). This is why you may feel pretty wired in the evenings and have difficulty waking up early the next morning. Especially when school start times are usually disgustingly early, meaning most teenagers don't get the recommended 8–10 hours' sleep they need. Yes, my friends, sleep deprivation governs our existence… what did we do to deserve this kind of torture! And to add fuel to the fire, our pesky little developing prefrontal cortex and hyperactive amygdala make bedtime the ideal time for overthinking—something the generation is an expert in! And the result? You guessed it—ANXIETY.

Don't worry, it's not all misery! We'll dive deeper into the science of sleep and share some useful tips to help you get better rest later in the book—so hang in there!

5.2 Connection Chaos (What Happens Socially)

Finding Your Place

Singer and songwriter Taylor Swift has opened up about how her experiences at school sparked a long-standing struggle with insecurity. She often felt like an outsider, never quite fitting in, and it was during this time that she first encountered the painful feeling of alienation.

Brain development is also related to social experiences at this stage of our lives. Self-perception and peer relationships are particularly important. A famous psychologist called Erik Erikson described this stage of development as 'identity vs role confusion' (Erikson, 1959). In other words—a period of self-discovery while also being worried about getting it wrong. Think about all the second-guessing, overthinking, not having it all figured out but feeling like you should, etc. It's fun, isn't it! There is light at the end of the tunnel, though. Identity is something that changes over time as we explore new things and step out of our comfort zone. Plot twist: you're not meant to have it all figured out yet. And don't worry—we'll come back to this later in the book, with lots of strategies to help you find your inner zen and feel more secure in the wonderful human you are!

As the brain's pre-frontal is developing (or the rooms are still being renovated in our house), we are also very conscious of avoiding social rejection from our peers. This means that we tend to take more risks as the social benefits outweigh the consequences of decisions (Pfeifer & Allen, 2021). The pressure to fit in and find your 'clique' is a relentless journey, demanding a lot of stamina. God forbid you lose your place in the constantly fluctuating pecking order of torment that school-aged students (mostly females, sorry girls!) fabricate for themselves. Fortunately, being Queen B in year 9 doesn't spark the same respect when you're 25, struggling to pay your rent.

It's no wonder that young people navigating this time in their lives respond to stress differently than older individuals, leading to an increased risk of developing anxiety or depression as we try to manage our growing brain (Arain et al., 2013). So it's particularly important during this time to prioritise self-care and practise strategies that calm us down. You're in the right place—this book is packed with practical examples and strategies to help you do just that.

Breaking Free

At this stage of our lives, we start to break away from the safety net of family and attempt to go at it alone! While this period is exciting, it can be very anxiety-provoking. We long to be able to make our own decisions but also aren't quite sure what choice we should make. We're overly worried about getting it perfect. Striking the right balance is near impossible, but we tend to put a lot of pressure on ourselves to get it 'right'. This transitional time is rooted in science. Remember, your brain is in the middle of its renovation or, should we say, serious revamp! The prefrontal cortex (which we know is responsible for decision-making and planning) is learning how to refine its skills through trial and error. Moments of self-doubt are part of the process, on the path to mastering the complexities of independence.

Having gone through my late teens/early twenties trying to perfect every life choice I made, I can truly empathise—it's no walk in the park. But I can promise you, it does get easier. As the years go by, you start to realise that the perfect choice doesn't exist—it's just the blind leading the blind. If you make it through the day in one piece, that's a massive win!!

> There's a sentiment expressed by actor Tom Hanks that in our twenties, we often search for a sense of purpose and direction—trying to find the place we're supposed to be. In our thirties, we start to see that meaning is rooted in **presence** more than **geography**.

Falling Hard, Overthinking Harder

As we reach middle adolescence, our brain becomes more advanced. Let's go back to our house renovation analogy: the rooms are starting to take shape, and you've added some big, double-glazed windows, symbolising new forms of social connection, namely romantic relationships, allowing a new outlook. You're not there yet—the plumbing still needs some work, and a few corners need polishing—but the house is starting to look like a home.

Real-Life Story: Izzy's First Love Jitters

Izzy had never felt anything like this before—the butterflies every time she saw Ben at school, the excitement when he first texted her and the warmth when he laughed at her seriously cringey jokes. Boys had always been a bit gross to her, until now.

But with the lust and joy came a certain jittery feeling. She constantly questioned whether she was good enough for him, and if he'd just get bored of her and move on to the next gangly, braced-up girl at school. Besides, she'd probably scare him away with one of her stupid comments at some point, she thought. She'd never cared so much about a single reply before, but now she overanalysed everything... even the way he greeted her and how many kisses he added at the end. It was mentally exhausting!! When she didn't get her morning text, her stomach twisted itself into knots. Had she been too boring? Too clingy? She second-guessed everything she said and did. Was first love meant to feel like this—half euphoria, half torment?!

Sit with the uncertainty of first love jitters; it may feel overwhelming now, but one day it'll fade, and you'll look back with a sense of growth, clarity and even fondness for the vulnerable person you once were!

5.3 Uncharted Waters *OR* New World, New Worries (What Happens Environmentally)

David Attenborough, broadcaster, biologist (...and national treasure!), has publicly acknowledge how engaged and aware young people are. He recognises that they understand the future of the planet will directly affects their lives.

Growing Up, Growing Crisis

Studies have shown that young people are becoming increasingly aware and worried about the impact of climate change, commonly known as climate anxiety or eco-anxiety. This isn't just a coincidence. Yes, there is greater awareness of our impending doom, but this type of anxiety also intersects with this particular developmental stage—a time for forging our identity and finding purpose. Think back to earlier in this section, when we talked about our growing brain.

That very brain is developing more abstract, critical thinking and consequently becoming more able to understand global challenges. If that weren't anxiety-provoking enough, social media and the news add their twopence, creating a sense of hysteria and responsibility that we inevitably take on as our own.

I don't know about you, but my late teens were a period of finding, and using, my voice… sometimes a little too much! As I started to develop a sense of agency, I started to challenge those around me—particularly my parents—about anything and everything. Quite literally! I recall picking a fight about their obsession with buying Evian plastic water bottles from the supermarket when they should be using reusable ones. No hate at Evian, they just weren't the most environmentally friendly option, and they caught a moody teenager on the wrong day! I guess what I'm trying to say here is that young adulthood is hard. We deal with a lot. We're trying to simultaneously balance and navigate personal uncertainty, raging hormones, a bigger brain, social ambiguity WHILST trying to solve the world's climate problems… that's no small feat. But I'm here to tell you, you're doing great. Cut yourself some slack and go with the flow—it's all worth it!

Real-Life Story: Lucian and the Weight of the World

With university around the corner, Lucian was entering a new and exciting time of his life. However, it didn't feel like that to him. All his friends were talking endlessly about dream jobs and travelling southeast Asia (if you know, you know!), but Lucian felt weighed down by the state of the world. Should he study finance, like his parents wanted, or follow his passion for conservation and sustainable development.

His parents didn't fully grasp that he was stepping into adulthood in a world far more uncertain than the one they had known. He didn't just want to sit around and wait for it to crumble before his eyes. He felt a duty to do something. He felt totally overwhelmed—how was he supposed to navigate all the conflicting opinions and expectations? It was too much to carry. Was there a way forward without feeling like he was failing both the people around him and the planet itself?

A+ Anxiety

No one warns you about the pressure to be exceptional academically. There I was, happy as Larry, mucking around with my mates in Year 8 with no care in the world. Then BOOM, GSCEs arrive, and I'm suddenly expected to actually do some work… I mean, the cheek of schoolteachers, right?!

This marked the start of a gruelling path to academic success, one where no matter how well I did, it never felt quite good enough. This pressure to succeed in the academic realm stems from the belief that we live in a society that rewards talent: the only acceptable path to success comes from hard work, perfect grades and a place at Oxbridge. Dr Daniel Markovits, author of *The Meritocracy Trap*, argues that this system has resulted in enormous psychological strain on young people as they strive for nothing short of perfection. The cost? Burnout, self-doubt, anxiety, to name just a few.

This is the world we live in—a system that thrives on us rarely feeling 'enough'. While it may not change overnight (or in our lifetimes!), it's important to remember that you're not alone. It's real and it's shared by so many others, even if they don't show it explicitly. We're all just trying to find our way in this relentless rat race. Be kind to yourself. Know that your self-worth is not measured by the amount of A*s you have, what university you go to, or even the length of time you spent procrastinating daily!

Helpful reminder: Jeremy Clarkson got a C and two Us at A-level. Now he's a multimillionaire with a car collection and a show about cows! Perspective is key.

The Price of Growing Up

If the climate crisis isn't enough of a worry, we've got the utter chaos of the current job market. Add that to the student debt and rising cost of living, it feels like a miracle just to make it through the day (especially living in London; who decided that was a good idea!?). I started 'adulthood' financially behind due to my outrageously high student debt, which I will continue to pay off for more years than I can count. And for what? It hasn't guaranteed me a good job, let alone a well-paying one. Then comes the comparison—which really is a nuisance! Sam's flying high, making six figures and throwing cash around like it's confetti on his Instagram page. Cheers Sam, I feel much better about myself now! This may be all a show for the 'gram', but it makes the financial struggles a hundred times worse.

It's a battlefield, friends, and I was down before the fight even began! This constant balancing act is not good for our cortisol levels, especially since we spent most of our lives till this point not having to worry about that stuff and leaving it to the oldies! Unlike older generations, we are often financially dependent on our parents for longer nowadays, which doesn't help our self-esteem and can amplify anxiety. Oh yeh, I almost forgot—AI is also stealing our jobs, so good luck finding one!

While job uncertainty and financial stress is totally valid, there are ways to take back control. Stick with me and we'll explore some practical strategies for overcoming the stress and keeping your head above water. Remember, you're never alone. So many people are feeling *exactly* the same way you are right now—questioning every choice they make and worrying about what's ahead. The good news? There's not any. JOKING. You don't need to have all the answers right now. You're growing older and wiser each day. It's meant to be a bit messy and overwhelming, but with each day you're learning and getting to grips with who *you* are and where you fit into this crazy world. And that's enough.

Reflect & Act: From Surviving to Thriving

Reflect:
- Do you feel like you should have it all figured out? Ask yourself: whose timeline am I following?

Act:
- Do one thing just because you enjoy it, not because it's productive.

The Bumpy Ride: You've Got This!

These changes are all part of growing up and growing wiser. Don't fight it, embrace it! It's a journey of navigating challenges, learning, and evolving. And don't worry—it gets easier. Later in the book, we'll dive into some life-style hacks to help you build resilience, stay strong, and make this period a little easier to navigate.

Key Takeaways

Before we move on, here's what to remember from this chapter:

- Adolescence is a very important time for the human brain. Throughout our teens, the brain is growing at a fast rate.
- The amygdala is very active in adolescence, making us more sensitive to emotional stimuli, which can foreshadow anxiety.
- Hormonal levels rise throughout adolescence, explaining the cascade of mood swings and emotional volatility.

- As the brain's pre-frontal lobe develops, we are very conscious of 'fitting in' and may take more risks, which can lead to mental health challenges.
- The state of the environment and economy are not helping our anxiety levels. But there are ways to take back control. Focusing on what you can control—like daily habits, mindset, and self-care—can help reduce overwhelm. Small steps can empower you to manage uncertainty.

Mission accomplished: Balancing Growth and Anxiety

Next stop: Now that you've navigated anxiety in the face of change, it's time to look at simple changes to your diet, exercise, sleep and screen time which can help boost your mental health and reduce anxiety. Get ready to spice up your life and discover a new you through a healthier lifestyle!

References

Arain, M., Haque, M., Johal, L., Mathur, P., Nel, W., Rais, A., Sandhu, R. & Sharma, S. (2013). Maturation of the adolescent brain. *Neuropsychiatric Disease and Treatment, 9*, 449–461. https://doi.org/10.2147/NDT.S39776.

Erikson, E. (1959). Theory of identity development. In *E. Erikson, Identity and the life cycle* (pp. 91–141). New York: International Universities Press.

Garcia, I. & O'Neil, J. (2021). Anxiety in adolescents. *The Journal for Nurse Practitioners, 17*(1), 49–53.

Hare, T. A., Tottenham, N., Galvan, A., Voss, H. U., Glover, G. H. & Casey, B. (2008). Biological substrates of emotional reactivity and regulation in adolescence during an emotional go-nogo task. *Biological Psychiatry, 63*(10), 927–934.

Hersh, C., Sisti, J., Richiutti, V. & Schernhammer, E. (2015). The effects of sleep and light at night on melatonin in adolescents. *Hormones, 14*, 399–409.

Markovits, D. (2019). *The meritocracy trap: How America's foundational myth feeds inequality, dismantles the middle class, and devours the elite.* Penguin Press.

Mousikou, M., Kyriakou, A. & Skordis, N. (2023). Stress and growth in children and adolescents. *Hormone Research in Paediatrics, 96*(1), 25–33.

Pfeifer, J. H. & Allen, N. B. (2021). Puberty initiates cascading relationships between neurodevelopmental, social, and internalizing processes across adolescence. *Biological Psychiatry, 89*(2), 99–108.

Raising Children Network. (2024). Child development: The first 5 years. https://raising-children.net.au/guides/first-1000-days/development/development-first-five-years.

Simpson, E. (2016). Carrying on with wayward sons: With their brains not maturing until their mid-20s, it's time to use a different approach to life and learning with our young men. *London Free Press.*

Tottenham, N. & Galván, A. (2016). Stress and the adolescent brain: Amygdala-prefrontal cortex circuitry and ventral striatum as developmental targets. *Neuroscience & Biobehavioral Reviews, 70*, 217–227.

Lifestyle Lifesavers
Simple Hacks for a Calmer You

All the hoo haa about
'small changes make a big difference'
isn't just talk after all!

Figure 6.1 A glimpse into my thoughts: a page from my personal journal.

Walter Anderson, American artist and author of The Confidence Course, *suggested that the best way to manage anxiety is to act. Doing something, however small, can break the vicious cycle.*

> **GOAL:** Provide practical lifestyle tips, such as improving diet, exercise, sleep and screen time habits, to help reduce anxiety and promote overall wellbeing.

Now that we have covered some of the fundamentals, I think it's time to share some small lifestyle changes that can make a big difference. We'll discover how a few tweaks to your diet, exercise routine, sleep regime and even screen use can help calm your mind and reduce your levels of anxiety. These essential habits are the first step in building a more resilient you. Sometimes, we just need to strip things back to basics and stop overcomplicating it. If you're sceptical, no worries—I'll back it up with scientific evidence! So, without further ado, let's get you acquainted with some epic lifestyle hacks to outsmart that pestering anxiety!

DOI: 10.4324/9781003670117-7

Before I offer you the tools to build your own anxiety toolkit, I'd like to provide a bit of context for these recommendations. What I didn't mention earlier is that a lot of my inspiration for writing this book came from my job as an assistant psychologist in the memory assessment service for the National Health Service. This is a specialised service for people aged 65+ who are experiencing memory problems. Its role is to conduct thorough assessments on patients to determine the nature and severity of memory issues, while also offering guidance and support to both them and their families. In my job, I encountered countless people with worsening cognitive decline—a great deal of which, I discovered, could have been prevented or at least delayed through simple but impactful lifestyle changes. Dementia is a cruel disease that, like anxiety, doesn't discriminate. Nearly everyone knows someone who has suffered from it. What many people don't know, however, is that adopting healthy habits early in life can decrease your risk of developing dementia. They don't teach you that at school or on Instagram, do they? Or at least when they do, it's too little too late.

So why is this relevant? Well, improving our brain health through positive lifestyle choices like exercise, good nutrition, and adequate sleep not only helps prevent conditions like dementia, but it can also reduce anxiety symptoms and help enhance our overall emotional resilience right now. In fact, there are many conditions which can be mitigated, if not entirely eradicated, by leading a healthy lifestyle. I'm not saying that if you lead a perfectly healthy life (which is impossible, by the way, as perfection is an illusion!) then you won't experience anxiety, dementia or any other conditions. I'm just saying that you will be doing yourself a great favour by at least practising healthy habits sooner rather than later.

As we go through the following topics, I'll be sharing evidence to show why each might be useful to be at least aware of when it comes to taking action to reduce anxiety. As mentioned before, some of these may be helpful for you and some may not. That's okay. We all have unique needs. Recognising these individual differences is vital for effectively managing anxiety and empowering yourself to take an active role in looking after your mental health.

This is **not** an exhaustive list. Though all of these *may* be helpful, if your anxiety is severe you may need to seek professional help. Please see Resources and Further Reading for more information on how to access this.

6.1 Can What I Eat Impact My Anxiety?

Now I know what you're thinking... We're constantly being told how important it is to eat our greens and avoid processed food. Bombarded by adverts on the latest healthy eating trends, superfoods and the food industry's biggest craze, PROTEIN. Frankly, it's tiresome and impossible to keep up with. Well, I'm not here to preach about the importance of a healthy diet; we have heard it all before. I'm just going to present the research evidence on how what we put into our body affects us when it comes to anxiety.

Like any other organ in the body, our brain is affected by our diet. Eating a healthy diet helps more oxygenated blood get to the brain, which allows brain cells to function better and means they are less likely to die (Barber & Sattar, 2021). Nutrient-dense foods (such as whole foods, vegetables and healthy fats) have less sugar than processed and sugary foods (such as fast-food and cake) and therefore your body's blood sugar levels remain steady rather than fluctuating dramatically. Eating nutritious foods also helps you to stay fuller for longer.[1] Processed foods on the other hand tend to lack essential nutrients, vitamins and minerals, which can affect your mood (Lane et al., 2022).

Not all sugar is bad, though. Consuming sugar through natural sources like fruit (as opposed to refined sugar) is good for you. Why? Natural sources of sugar have a similar effect as nutrient-dense foods do in that they keep your metabolism stable (Stanhope, 2016). They also contain fibre, which stops spikes in blood sugar levels as it moves slowly through the body, helping you stay fuller for longer.

PRO TIP: Plan and prepare your meals in advance to avoid unhealthy choices.

Brain Boost

A review of 45 studies explored how diet affected the mental health of university students. Out of these, 36 studies found that students eating a healthy, balanced diet experienced better mental health, including lower levels of anxiety, depression and overall stress. And it doesn't stop there—the review also found that poor, unbalanced diets were linked to elevated stress and anxiety levels in students. This shows that eating well can actually help protect you from mental health difficulties (Solomou et al., 2023)!

The hormone cortisol is produced in our adrenal glands (located on top of our kidneys) and is referred to as the body's 'stress hormone'. This is because levels of cortisol increase when we're stressed (Cay et al., 2018). Cortisol is important in suitable amounts, but when it's too high for prolonged periods it can be harmful for the body in many different ways, including mood disorders, increased risk of heart disease, lowered immunity (to name a few). Research suggests that certain foods can help reduce cortisol levels (García & Hernández, 2020; Werner-Gray, 2020). Below are a few examples that you may want to consider incorporating into your diet. (REMEMBER, eating these foods does not mean that you will live a life devoid of anxiety, or other health issues, it is merely a way of better regulating your body's cortisol levels and improving your mental and physical wellbeing.)

Some suggestions:

1. **Fatty fish** → rich in omega-3 fatty acids which have anti-inflammatory properties and reduce the levels of cortisol created in the body (van Zonneveld, 2024).
2. **Dark chocolate** → contains antioxidants which help reduce levels of cortisol. One study examined the effect of dark chocolate on the body's stress response. Healthy (non-smoking) males were assigned to either a dark chocolate group or a placebo group. After eating the chocolates, they participated in a psychosocial stress task. Their stress hormone levels were measured before and after the task. Results showed a significantly weakened reactivity of cortisol in the dark chocolate eating group compared to the placebo group, which led researchers to conclude that dark chocolate reduces cortisol, which is associated with reduced stress (Wirtz et al., 2014).[2]
3. **Fruits** → High in vitamin C, antioxidants and other nutrients that help stabilise cortisol levels. As mentioned earlier, cortisol is produced in our adrenal glands; these glands contain a lot of vitamin C and therefore when we eat foods rich in vitamin C, we are keeping them nourished (Urizar et al., 2021).

Snack smart: Opt for nuts, seeds or fruit over processed, sugary snacks to help regulate your cortisol levels.

Brain Boost

The role of cortisol isn't limited to the body's stress response. It helps regulate our immune system and metabolism, controls blood sugar levels, and is involved in our circadian rhythm (our sleep-wake cycle, more on which later).

How Does Gut Health Reduce Anxiety?

Did you know that stress can affect your gut health? Think back to a time when you felt nervous and it caused you to have, for want of a better phrase, a 'nervous poo'? This isn't just a coincidence. There's a direct link between your thoughts and your gut. Increased levels of stress can cause 'intestinal permeability', also known as 'leaky gut'. This causes food to pass through the intestinal lining and into our bloodstream (Varanoske et al., 2022).

I'll pause here to introduce you to one of my closest friends, let's call her Julie, whose anxiety caused a host of less-than-convenient stomach issues. She readily made a joke about it to those around her, but I knew how debilitating it was. During one of our frequent five-hour natters, she shared a deeper account of her experience.

Julie's Inner Storm

Anxiety completely took over Julie's life for a year. It started off slowly and, looking back, she probably knew it was building, given the change that was occurring in her life at that time. However, suddenly it was so overwhelming that it stopped her doing all the things she had previously taken for granted. The biggest thing it affected was her physical health. She had always been someone with stomach problems, but her anxiety made this an everyday problem that stopped her from leaving the house without knowing where the nearest toilet or escape route was. Consequently, she never wanted to be too far from home, and this had a huge impact on her social life, and ultimately her mood. She felt so out of control, and she found it increasingly difficult to speak about at the time.

She was so attuned to every sensation in her body, catastrophising and misinterpreting it completely. Having studied psychology for years, she frequently talked to her own clients about this, but no amount of knowledge could help her change the vicious cycle that was playing out between her body and her thoughts. It wasn't until she got psychological support and a specialist dietician's input that things started to improve. And she came to appreciate, for the first time, the impact of sleep, diet and routine on both her physical health and mental health. Sometimes she finds it hard talking in the mental health field about the experiences she's had, feeling like she should have known this at the time. However, it has also made her appreciate even more how quickly things can spiral and that anxiety can impact anyone. Sometimes we might know the triggers, a specific situation or experience, but other times it may creep up on us slowly until suddenly you're in the thick of it and it feels like you can't turn back.

Chronic stress is in fact a key factor in the development of IBS, a bowel disorder affecting an astonishing 10 to 20 per cent of the population. It's only recently that researchers have identified the importance of psychological factors in the activation and maintenance of symptoms. Many people are advised to start the low FODMAP diet, a dietary plan to reduce symptoms (Tang et al., 2021). Alternatively, some are advised to try psychotherapy, because of the involvement of psychological factors in digestive problems.

PRO TIP: Slow down and chew your food thoroughly! Take time to chew your food well for better digestion and to prevent overeating.

How Can We Improve Our Own Gut Health?

You've probably heard this a thousand times before, but the fact remains that incorporating a colourful array of foods (a.k.a. 'the rainbow') into our diet can help improve our gut health by increasing the diversity of our gut microbes. This in turn nourishes our brain and body, helping us fight diseases and improve our overall health and wellbeing (Blumfield et al., 2022).

The foods we need for this include:

Nutrients: Colourful fruits and vegetables contain many nutrients and vitamins, e.g. an orange provides vitamin C while green vegetables like kale provide magnesium.

Fibre: Many foods, particularly fruits and vegetables, are rich in fibre which is vital to maintaining healthy digestion.

Antioxidants: Many colourful foods, such as berries and purple cabbage, contain antioxidants like flavonoids which reduce inflammation of the bowel.

Phytochemicals: These are compounds found in plant-based foods. By eating 'the rainbow' you are ensuring a variety of phytochemicals enter your gut which helps to maintain a healthy gut microbiome (Deis et al., 2021).

PRO TIP: Aim to balance your plate with a mix of protein, carbs and healthy fats in each meal.

The Eatwell Plate (see Figure 6.2 on the next page) was first introduced by the UK government's Food Standards Agency (FSA) in 2007 to help people understand how to balance different food groups to achieve a balanced diet. In 2016, it was updated in line with nutritional guidelines and renamed the 'Eatwell Guide' by Public Health England (2016).

1. **Fruits and vegetables:** should make up approximately one-third of your diet. *Aim for 5 portions per day*
2. **Carbs and starches:** including bread, pasta, rice should make up approximately one-third of your diet. *Opt for wholegrain or high-fibre options.*
3. **Proteins:** including fish, eggs, chickpeas and meats should make up approximately one-sixth of your plate. *Variety is key here. Be curious and experimental!*
4. **Dairy (and alternatives):** including milk, cheese, yogurt, and plant-based alternatives. *Opt for low sugar options where possible*
5. **Sugars and fats:** including chocolate, sweets, cakes. These can be enjoyed in moderation as part of a balanced diet but should make up a smaller proportion of your plate.

Limit foods high in fat, salt, and sugar, and try to consume these less often and in small amounts.

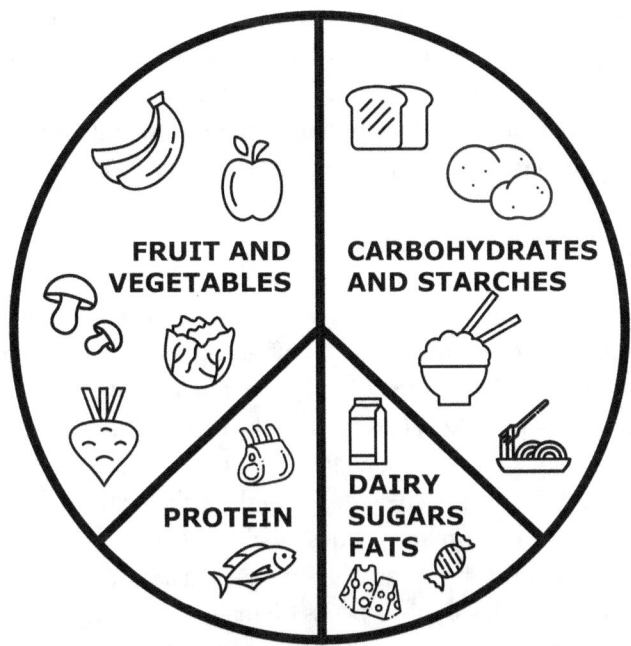

Figure 6.2 Adapted from the Eatwell Guide, © Crown copyright [2016], used under the Open Government Licence v3.0.

How Does Water Reduce Anxiety?

Staying hydrated is an easy way to reduce anxiety and helps our brain and body function properly. How? Well, surprisingly a whopping 75 per cent of our brain tissue is made up of water (Oros-Peusquens et al., 2019). Just 2 per cent dehydration can cause us to feel tired and lethargic and impair our mood. This is because when we're dehydrated, the brain is unable to produce as much energy, causing it to slow down. Cortisol levels also increase when we are dehydrated, which, as we've already learnt, increases anxiety (Zaplatosch & Adams, 2020).

Many studies have shown an association between dehydration and elevated anxiety levels. For example, one study conducted in 2022 examined the relationship between hydration and anxiety levels among 65 female university students in Spain. They found those with insufficient fluid intake showed higher levels of anxiety, highlighting the importance of adequate hydration on mental wellbeing (Castro-Alija et al., 2023).

PRO TIP: Start your morning with a glass of water and try sipping little and often throughout the day. The NHS Eatwell Guide recommends drinking 1.5 litres per day. Don't take it too far, though, as drinking too much water can also be dangerous (take that for information overload!). But rest assured that drinking to thirst and around 1.5 litres per day won't kill you!

How Does Caffeine Impact Anxiety?

Caffeine is the most popular psychoactive drug in the world. When most people think of caffeine, they think of coffee and tea. However, many other things contain it, including fizzy drinks, chocolate and some medication. Caffeine has many positive effects, such as increased alertness and attention, which is why many people drink coffee in the morning to wake them up and kick start the day. There is even evidence to show that caffeine has a positive impact on sporting performance (Guest et al., 2021).

It's important to know, however, that some people are more affected or sensitive to caffeine than others. This depends on many factors including the body's ability to metabolise caffeine, counter effects of certain medications, genetic vulnerabilities, age, and drug/alcohol consumption (Rodak et al., 2021).

> ### Brain Boost
>
> Did you know that caffeine-induced anxiety disorder is recognised as a distinct condition in the *Diagnostic and Statistical Manual of Mental Disorders (DSM-5-TR)*? It is described as 'anxiety and panic attacks caused directly by the consumption of caffeine' (American Psychiatric Association, 2013).

Do you ever feel more anxious in the morning than other parts of the day? Do you experience feelings of worry, muscle tension, racing thoughts or light-headedness? This may be due to the fact that cortisol (mentioned previously) is at its highest the hour after you first wake up. Cortisol helps us to wake up from sleep. This can be tricky if you already experience anxiety, as your cortisol levels will already be at a heightened state first thing. And, to top things off, most people reach for coffee to wake them up, but this worsens anxiety further. I'm not saying don't drink coffee (I'm mildly obsessed), but just be careful as you may be somebody who is particularly susceptible to its contents combined with a more anxious brain.

Let's bring the facts to life and jump into a real-life example with a real person! What's even more meaningful is that this person is someone very close to me, and her journey with anxiety had a profound impact on my decision to write this book.

Annie's Caffeine Jitters

Annie, a 20-something sales assistant, loved waking up to her oat flat whites in the morning. For years she consumed 3–4 cups of coffee a day to stay energised amidst a hectic schedule. Recently, she began feeling increasingly jittery and irritable, struggling to focus on tasks. She realised that her anxiety symptoms, including a pounding heart and racing thoughts, often peaked after her morning coffee routine. After much deliberation, Annie decided to take a brave step and experiment with her caffeine intake by switching to decaffeinated coffee (decaf oat flat whites taste just as good—just saying!). Lo and behold, it didn't harm her, nor did it disrupt her life. In just two weeks, Annie noticed a significant decrease in her anxiety levels. She felt calmer throughout the day, her mind felt much clearer and sharper, and her sleep improved too! And you know what? Five years later, she's still drinking decaf. Don't be fooled—she still experiences anxiety from time to time, which is normal. However, by reducing her caffeine intake, she significantly lowered the chances of a flare-up. She controlled the controllables. This example illustrates how even moderate amounts of caffeine can contribute to increased anxiety symptoms in some people.

How Does Caffeine Affect the Body?

Caffeine indirectly stimulates the release into the bloodstream of chemicals like dopamine, serotonin, and norepinephrine, which are associated with feelings of pleasure. This can cause an increase in our blood pressure, leading to a faster heart rate and potentially worsening feelings of anxiety (Sharma et al., 2023).

Additionally, caffeine triggers the production of stress hormones, such as cortisol and epinephrine, which can cause blood sugar levels to drop, making you feel irritable and confused while further increasing your heart rate (Sabaei et al., 2022).

Moreover, caffeine blocks the uptake of gamma-aminobutyric acid (GABA), a neurotransmitter that promotes feelings of calm. It also leads to the loss of essential nutrients which are vital for mood regulation and overall brain health (Sharma et al., 2023). Consequently, the effect of caffeine can be likened to a frightening situation where the body's fight or flight response is activated, as outlined earlier. Now, this is by no means intended to put you off caffeine or scare you about its effects. I'm an avid coffee drinker, but that's because I am one of the lucky ones who isn't as sensitive to it as some people are (at least at the present moment!). This information is only a guide, just in case caffeine could be contributing to or exacerbating your anxiety levels. If this is so, perhaps switching to decaf or sticking to one coffee per day in the late morning/midday (when cortisol levels have depleted somewhat) might be a good idea? Trial it and see how it goes? With coffee prices approaching £5 these days, I might have just saved you a small fortune. You can thank me later …

Remember, many fizzy drinks contain caffeine, so just be aware of this!

The Key Ingredients for Anxiety Relief

Why not try the following simple strategies to help reduce your anxiety and improve your overall wellbeing:

1. Staying hydrated is so important! Try drinking 1.5 litres of water per day.
2. Reduce your caffeine intake and limit this to mornings (especially if you have an anxious temperament!).
3. Try introducing/increasing foods in your diet that reduce cortisol levels (e.g. salmon, dark chocolate, fruits).
4. Don't miss meals (or your energy levels will pay the price!).
5. Try to match your plate to the 'Eatwell Plate' and eat the rainbow!
6. Avoid over-consumption of refined sugar (remember, it's about balance/ moderation not elimination).

6.2 Can Exercise Help Tame My Anxiety?

It's all well and good saying *'do more exercise'* but what we really want to know is WHY? It doesn't take a genius to realise that physical exercise helps our physical health, but up until recently little was known about the benefits of movement on our mental health. Let's look at some of the biology to help us understand why this is the case. Maybe then you'll be more inclined to put it into practice!

You may have heard of endorphins before. They're chemical messengers in the brain that help the body avoid pain and increase pleasure, also known as the 'feel good' chemical. A shortage of endorphins can contribute to feelings of stress. You might wonder why some people take drugs? Certain drugs activate the release of endorphins, leading to feelings of pleasure. This creates a desire to continue using (or abusing) them (Zheng, 2022). Endorphins are also released when we exercise, serving as a natural way of raising endorphin levels and reducing the likelihood of stress, thereby stimulating the same positive effects as a drug (Ali et al., 2021).

It's time for another real-life example, and once again, my mum is in the spotlight—she's really stealing the show!

Run, Mum, Run!

Ever since I was a little girl, my mum has been a huge advocate of running. When my dad fell seriously ill, she ran every single morning, come rain or shine. She simply couldn't start her day any other way and would be a bit of a nightmare (sorry mum!) on the rare occasion she had to miss one due to an appointment or ill health. I guess you could say it was somewhat of an addiction. When I was young, I couldn't comprehend why someone would want to run once a month let alone every single day. I was concerned that she might have become overly fixated on her physical fitness. However, over time I got to the core of her obsession. Though she was conscious of the benefits to her physical wellbeing, the main reason was mental. Running gave my mum time to clear her head and find relief from her anxious thoughts. Now that I'm older I can completely understand. She had to juggle the emotional turmoil of caring for her severely ill husband, managing three squabbling kids, and balance work and home life, all of which must have been unimaginably stressful. Running was her outlet. Her safe space. Running gave her a chance to relieve feelings of overwhelm, allowing her to show up fully for her family.

Although it pains me to admit it, I think my mum was on to something. Over the last few years, I have taken up running. At first, it was just to maintain my physical health, but it has become increasingly more about the positive benefits it has had on my mental health. When I feel stressed or worried about anything, running is my therapy. I guess daughters do take after their mothers after all!!

PRO TIP: Set a phone reminder to move every hour during your workday for a quick stretch or walk.

The mental health benefits of exercise aren't just a coincidence; there's a scientific, brain-based reason behind them.

What Exactly Happens When We Exercise?

When our heart rate increases, there is an increase in the activation of essential neurochemicals such as serotonin, GABA and endocannabinoids, which help reduce anxiety and enhance our sense of wellbeing. So, exercise literally changes our brain chemistry.

I've included a brief definition of each of these neurochemicals and how they're important when it comes to the biochemistry of anxiety.

- **Serotonin:** a chemical which helps regulate/modulate mood, sleep and digestion.
- **Gamma aminobutyric acid (GABA):** a chemical which plays an important role in calming down the brain by slowing cell hyperactivity associated with anxiety and stress.
- **Endocannabinoids:** a chemical which helps to control critical bodily functions including emotional processing and sleep.

(Ruiz-Tejada et al., 2022)

Brain Boost

Researchers investigated the influence of endorphins on the stress response of mice. They evaluated the behaviour of mice at different levels of endorphin (β-E). They found a direct relationship between endorphin levels and anxious behaviour, suggesting endorphins moderate the response to stressful stimuli in mice (Grisel, Bartels, Allen, & Turgeon, 2008).

Quick Win: Stand up, stretch, and take five big, deep breaths—your body and mind will thank you!

Exercise, Inflammation, and Anxiety: Interconnections and Implications

Exercise influences our body's stress hormones, the major one being cortisol (which we've already covered). Regular exercise helps lower resting cortisol levels over time, helping us to manage stress better.

Regular exercise has also been found to have anti-inflammatory effects, which is important in reducing anxiety and depression. It does this by activating immune cells (called Tregs) in our muscles, which helps fight inflammation while strengthening our body's ability to use energy and its immune function response (Rosa-Neto et al., 2022). Just 20 minutes of exercise per day can decrease the body's inflammatory response (Hsu et al., 2017).

Incorporating regular exercise into our routine can therefore play a crucial role in reducing inflammation and anxiety by strengthening our stress-coping mechanisms, enhancing physical health and improving wellbeing.

Guidelines for Exercise

The UK National Health Service (NHS) recommends that young people aged 5 to 18 do at least 60 minutes of moderate to vigorous intensity aerobic activity per day and adults aged 19 to 64 do a minimum of 150 minutes of moderate intensity exercise per week (NHS, 2021).

Remember, exercise isn't just running, football, weights… it could be an activity like cycling, Frisbee, Pilates etc. It doesn't have to be much either—a 15 min walk is great!! Anything that makes you move your body has many positive effects on the brain and body. If you can get out in the fresh air this is a BONUS.

PRO TIP: If you're struggling with motivation, consider joining a fitness class or group to turn exercise into a social activity.

6.3 Will Better Sleep Ease My Anxiety?

When I say I can't sleep because of anxiety, I don't mean I'm staying up worrying. I mean my body physically won't let me sleep.

Anonymous

It's time to talk about sleep. To be honest with you, before my roles in the NHS, sleep didn't much cross my mind. I mean, I knew it was important and that I loved a good lie-in, but I didn't think it could be so intrinsically linked to my health and wellbeing. In every patient assessment, whether in the memory assessment service or with mental health support services, I have been instructed to ask about sleep: how much did they get on average per night and was their sleep disturbed or not, etc. It is really quite alarming how many people are getting a dismal amount each night. In the memory assessment service, some of those who were diagnosed with Mild Cognitive Impairment (MCI) were offered a course revolving around maintaining good brain health. As poor sleep is a risk factor for dementia, as well as conditions like diabetes, cardiovascular disease, chronic pain, and mental health disorders, it featured as a stand-alone section. We referred to it as 'sleep hygiene' and provided various tips and tricks to help improve people's sleep, some of which I'll outline here.

You may be wondering why I'm giving you sleep tips found in an older people's memory service handbook? Firstly, sleep affects our mood. We often blame a lack of sleep for our being in a bad mood. Think back to a day when you got barely any sleep the night before; I'm sure you weren't your most delightful self! Second, the sleep tips I obtained from the memory service were designed to help reduce cognitive decline but are just as effective for reducing anxiety and a host of other conditions. Sleep is vital for human functioning and by actively appreciating its importance, you can help yourself in a number of ways. Moreover, what works for older people can also help younger people.

It's funny how, as kids, we see sleep as a punishment, but as we grow older, we realise it's actually a true gift!

Many of the tips I'm about to provide you with have helped my clients, colleagues, family members and friends alike. But before we dive into the science of sleep, let's kick things off with a real-life example from a friend of mine—let's call her Tilly.

Tilly's Midnight Struggle with Anxiety

Tilly, a high-achieving medical professional, began experiencing anxiety in her mid-20s due to pressures at work. As her anxiety grew, she noticed significant problems falling and staying asleep. She would lie awake for hours, unable to quieten her racing thoughts, and when she did eventually drift off, she often woke multiple times and struggled to return to sleep. This fragmented sleep left her feeling exhausted and agitated, impacting all aspects of her life. She couldn't focus on work tasks, she was too tired to go out with friends in the evening, and she noticed that she was getting ill frequently.

After struggling with these issues for longer than she wanted to admit, she put her foot down. Enough was enough. Her sleep issues were not going to govern her life anymore. Determined to find a solution, she began educating herself about sleep hygiene using online resources. She discovered some free techniques (we'll get to these soon, so hang tight!) that improved her sleep and helped her regain control over her anxiety and overall wellbeing. Remember, being well-rested can improve your mood and energy levels, helping you feel recharged.

PRO TIP: Try using an app like 'Headspace', which offers varying sleep exercises to suit every type of sleeper! In the 'Sleep' section you can find guided meditations, sleep sounds and bedtime stories designed to help you fall asleep more easily. The 'Sleepcasts' are great for unwinding before bed.

6.4 Why Does My Sleep Pattern Matter for My Anxiety?

The Importance of Sleep

Sleep is an essential body process, affecting our mental and physical wellbeing. It is a crucial time to refresh and reboot our brain and body. Getting consistent, good quality sleep helps a multitude of things.

1. When we sleep our body carries out vital repairs, such as building bone and muscles (Nobari et al., 2023).
2. When we sleep, our brain processes information and consolidates memories, helping our cognitive functioning and performance (Desai et al., 2024).

3. Sleeping aids the maintenance of a healthy heart and regulates our metabolism (Moosavi-Movahedi et al., 2021).
4. In adolescence, sleep is vital for growth, as the body's growth hormone is primarily secreted during sleep (Baranwal et al., 2023).
5. A healthy sleep pattern helps regulate our mood and emotional reactions (Groeger et al., 2022).

Brain Boost

Did you know that lack of sleep can affect your gut health? This is because our hormones become disturbed when we don't get enough sleep, causing an increase in the stress hormone cortisol. (You know the drill by now!)

To understand what happens when we sleep, you need to know that we move between two types of sleep, called Rapid Eye Movement (REM) sleep and non-Rapid Eye Movement (non-REM) sleep, throughout the night.

- **Non-REM** occurs predominantly at the start of our sleep cycle (i.e. for most people, the start of the night) where there are phases of light and deep sleep.
- **REM** sleep occurs predominantly later in our sleep cycle. This is when we experience rapid eye movements and may have dreams.

Both REM and non-REM sleep are vital for different aspects of physical and emotional wellbeing. In short, non-REM sleep is important for physical restoration and memory consolidation, while REM sleep helps regulate emotions and enhances cognitive functioning (Kaida et al., 2023). Deficiencies in either type can affect our overall health.

Why Does Sleep Affect Anxiety?

It's common for those with anxiety, whether temporary or chronic, to experience sleep problems (Chellappa & Aeschbach, 2022). Can you think of a time when you had an exam the next day and you struggled to sleep? The worry about the event caused your mind to race/ruminate about concerns and kept you awake… it always happens when you need sleep most, right? Sleep deprivation can also worsen anxiety, for instance by increasing the time the brain is fearful of a future event, causing an ongoing negative cycle. By being aware of the role that sleep plays in anxiety, we can better understand how best to address the problem and enhance our wellbeing.

Lack of sleep alters the flow to the brain of chemicals which are vital in regulating our mood. Let's take a look at each in turn (you may recognise these):

- **Serotonin:** A lack of sleep leads to a reduction in serotonin, the 'feel good' hormone, which leads to increased anxiety and irritability (Portas et al., 2000).
- **Dopamine:** A lack of sleep can reduce dopamine activity. Dopamine plays a key role in the brain's reward system, which helps regulate our mood, and lack of dopamine can leave us feeling lethargic (Klumpers et al., 2015).
- **Cortisol:** A lack of sleep causes a spike in cortisol levels, which is associated with increased anxiety and stress (Wright et al., 2015).
- **GABA:** A lack of sleep can lead to impaired GABA function, which causes increased anxiety and stress (Park et al., 2020).
- **Endocannabinoids:** Lack of sleep can cause changes to our endocannabinoid levels. As endocannabinoids are involved in our stress response, this can lead to increased levels of anxiety and stress (D'Angelo & Steardo, 2024).

PRO TIP: Smiling—even if it's forced—can trick your brain into feeling better. It's something called the 'facial feedback hypothesis', whereby the act of smiling activates the brain's reward system, releasing natural mood boosters like dopamine and serotonin (Ekman & Davidson, 1993).

The Sleep Science Scoop: How to Snooze like a Pro

Here are some simple guidelines to help with lower your anxiety levels through getting a good night's sleep.

1. **Create a regular sleep schedule**
   Try to be consistent with the times you go to bed and wake up (even at weekends!) as this will help regulate the body's internal clock.

2. **Devise a bedtime routine**

   Creating a relaxing bedtime routine is key to signalling to your body that it's time to wind down. You may want to take a hot bath, read a book, drink a decaf herbal tea or do some stress-reduction techniques. Oh, and avoid screens (you'll thank me later!).

3. **Check your sleep environment**

   It is important that the room where you sleep is actually conducive to sleep. There may be things in your surroundings that may exacerbate sleep difficulties, such as too much light in the bedroom or it's too warm or cold. Everyone's different. Find out what works for you and be consistent.

4. **Limit your screentime**

   Turn off screens an hour or so before bedtime, as blue light affects sleep quality (more on this later).

5. **Keep an eye on your diet!**

   I hope by this point you're not too surprised to learn that diet plays a crucial role in sleep hygiene. In particular, avoiding caffeine and alcohol before bedtime can have a huge impact on the quality of your sleep.

Let's take a look at why…

Reduce caffeine: Oh no, here we go again! To explain the effect of caffeine on sleep, it's helpful to understand what a 'half-life' means. In simple terms, a half-life is the time it takes for a substance to reduce to half of its initial amount. This concept is most often used when talking about radioactive materials in chemistry and physics. Caffeine has a half-life of 6 hours (Grant et al., 2023). This means that if you have a coffee at 12pm, then at midnight a quarter of the caffeine will still be in your system, interfering with the quality of your sleep. This may explain why you have trouble falling to sleep. If you are someone who struggles to sleep, why not try to resist consuming caffeine four to six hours from bedtime and see if you notice an improvement in your sleep?

Reduce alcohol: Many people think that having a drink before bed will help them fall asleep and have a better night's rest. While alcohol may help you fall asleep faster (as it acts as a sedative), it affects the later, deeper stages of sleep, also known as REM sleep (see above; Gardiner et al., 2024). This causes you to feel more 'groggy' and tired in the morning. To add fuel to the fire, alcohol can cause you to wake up more frequently during the night as its sedative effects wear off; and, due to its being a diuretic, it can increase the need for a trip to the loo, which further increases wakefulness.

Brain Boost

The effects of alcohol don't stop there. Research has shown that as little as four drinks per week can cause neurodegeneration in the brain, which is essentially when the cells of neurons die off. Consumption of alcohol affects our dopamine system, causing volatile highs and lows, which is why you may feel anxious (a.k.a. hangxiety) and lower in mood the day after a drinking session. I'm not saying don't drink alcohol. I'm saying be aware of the effects it's likely to have on the quality of your sleep and anxiety levels, and try not to drink a lot in the evenings.

Regular alcohol consumption, especially in large quantities, can disrupt our body's internal clock, known as the 'circadian rhythm'. Our circadian rhythm regulates physiological processes which are vital for our health and wellbeing (Desai et al., 2024). One that is well regulated promotes stronger mental health. A disturbed circadian rhythm, however, can result in various mood disorders such as depression and anxiety. Let's take a look at it in more detail in the following section.

6. **Be aware of light's effect on your body clock**
   Our circadian rhythm is basically our internal body clock which runs on a 24-hour cycle. It helps us align our body with the environment, responding to light and dark, so our brain can signal when to sleep, wake, eat, etc., and how much of each we need. Sometimes, our usual cycle becomes out of sync, for example when we're jetlagged. When we experience jetlag, our internal body clock is discordant with the local day–night cycle, causing us to be alert during the night/dark and sleepy in the day (Foster, 2022).

   Exposure to light plays a crucial role in regulating our circadian rhythm. Utilising a bright light alarm, for instance, gradually increases light intensity throughout the morning, so when you eventually wake you feel more rested and alert. Additionally, incorporating a lightbox into your daily routine, especially during darker seasons like winter, can boost light exposure. This in turn supports your circadian rhythm and prepares the body for rest when darkness falls (Yin et al., 2021).

Brain Boost

To provide some context, natural sunlight offers around 100,000 lux of illumination, while indoor lighting typically ranges from 30 to 500 lux. How shocking is that! This highlights the importance of seeking alternative light sources when sunlight exposure is limited. Using a lightbox, which typically emits 10,000 lux, may be a good way to achieve this. While it doesn't *fully* replace natural sunlight, a lightbox maintains regular light exposure, particularly during winter times (or summer if you live in the UK!), ensuring adequate light intake.

Morning light has the strongest influence on our body clock. Engaging in outdoor activities like walking, running or simply sitting in the garden early on in the day strengthens the body's internal clock, thereby promoting better sleep quality at night.

7. **Practise stress-reduction techniques**
   Practising stress-reduction techniques like mindfulness, meditation and breathing exercises can help calm your mind before bed, improving both your sleep and anxiety levels (Yegane et al., 2024). We'll take a closer look at these in the next chapter.

PRO TIP: 'Cognitive shuffling' is a technique developed by cognitive scientist Dr Luc P. Beaudoin (2014). After struggling with insomnia, he came up with an idea to help quieten the mind. It involves focusing on a neutral object and breaking it down, to distract your brain and facilitate sleep. Start by picking an object, like a chair or table, and with each letter of the word, think of a word that starts with it (e.g. for 'CHAIR', you may think: 'C = Cow, H = Ham, A = Apple, I = Ice, R = Rice). Focus on the words rather than the meanings, visualising each word briefly.

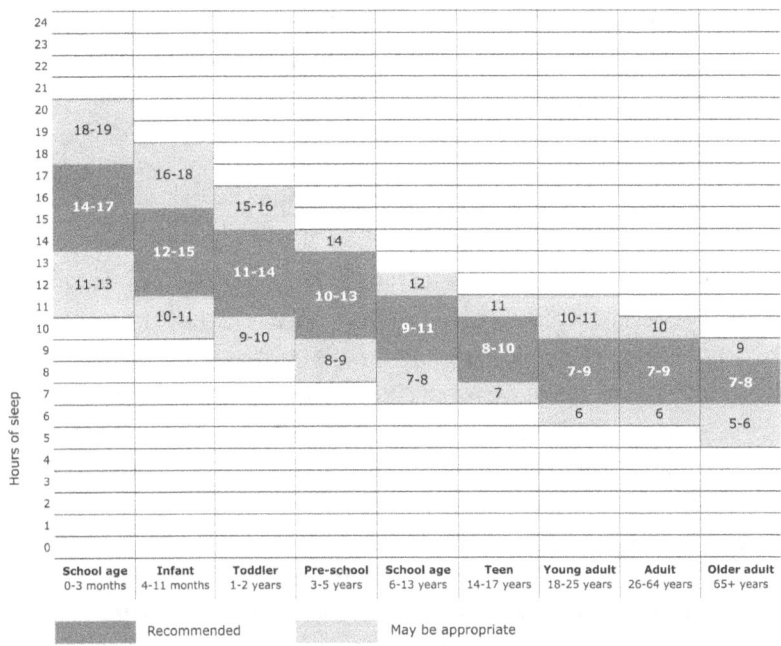

Figure 6.3 A visual guide to recommended sleep durations by age group, from newborns to older adults.

Ok, Point Made! So, How Much Sleep Do I Need?

The amount of sleep a person needs varies depending on their age (and other factors). See Figure 6.3 for a rough idea on sleep duration based on age, with the amount of sleep needed decreasing with age.

6.5 Can Too Much Screen Time Increase My Anxiety?

Technology, with its promises of connection, can sometimes drive us deeper into disconnection and anxiety.

Sherry Turkle, psychologist

Ever find yourself scrolling mindlessly through Instagram? Yep, guilty as charged! Multiple times a day I'd find myself watching some stranger's *'what I eat in a day'* or *'a day in the life'* reels, which largely consisted of watching them fold laundry or buy some avocados from Waitrose. When did we start enjoying watching other people do their housework? (Yes, I'm lumping us together to ease the self-shame!) To my parents, the idea is completely alien. 'Do you have nothing better to do?' they'd say, to which I'd respond, 'No, Kate, I don't actually.' But, after some time reflecting, I've realised that most of the time I scroll, it's to relieve boredom or avoid thinking about something distressing. But what does that really do? It just pushes the emotions and feelings further down, without actually addressing them in a productive way. Facing our feelings and the present moment can be scary, but it's necessary for growth.

I know, I know! It is hard to quantify how often my parents have told me to get off my phone. However frustrating it may have been, they had a point! There is this pervasive feeling that if we're not checking our phones 24/7 we are missing out on something. There is also an expectation that if a message is sent, it's read immediately and therefore a response should be too. We live in a new 'now'. This creates an unhealthy attachment with our phones and increases anxiety. In fact, research has consistently demonstrated a link between persistent mobile phone use and increased anxiety. This is quite alarming considering the average mobile phone user in the UK in 2024 spends over 4 to 5 hours PER DAY on their mobile phones, an increase of 3.7 hours from 2020 (Hunter, 2024). This was undoubtedly affected by the pandemic but doesn't seem to have wavered since and, given that the number of smartphone users is increasing year upon year, it doesn't seem likely to in the future either.

Screen Time Can Be Scream Time!

Brain Boost

Professor Jon Elhai, a specialist in cyberpsychology and internet addictions, conducted a systematic review of 23 peer-reviewed papers and found a relationship between problematic smartphone use and anxiety, such that the more people use their phones, the more likely they are to report anxiety and stress. There are many questions as to whether phone use and anxiety is a cause or effect relationship (i.e. is it the mobile phone addiction causing the anxiety *or* is it the anxiety causing the mobile phone addiction?). Regardless, the correlation itself shows that smartphone addiction is not productive for anxiety and any measures to reduce its consumption are likely to have a positive effect on anxiety (Elhai et al., 2017).

PRO TIP: A few simple changes can make a big difference. Why not swap scrolling for reading a new book, doing a mindfulness exercise, taking a walk or enjoying a good bubble bath!

Let's look at some of the reasons for this:

- **Blue light:** sleep is regulated by the hormone melatonin. When blue light is emitted by screens, the body's production of melatonin is disrupted, which affects the quality of our sleep. As we've already discussed in the sleep chapter, poor sleep is associated with increased anxiety (Silvani et al., 2022).
- **Dependence:** the expectation to always be available can disrupt your routine and create anxiety. Similarly, the gratification people get from checking apps/likes can become stressful and compulsive.
- **Physical health:** staring at a screen for too long can cause eye strain, headaches and discomfort, which may lead to anxiety (Fazal et al., 2024).
- **FOMO:** I'm sure you've all heard of this before, but I'll spell it out for those who slept through the 21st century. 'Fear of missing out' is increased by the pressure to stay up to date with every event or party, especially when such events are glamorised, leading to feelings of inadequacy and anxiety.

It's all well and good telling you to reduce your phone consumption, but if the content you do view is negative and harmful, it's not going to have the desired effect (i.e. reduce your anxiety levels). The fact is that we live in a comparison culture, one in which the algorithms are serving constantly to make us feel inadequate. Following influencers who're trying to sell products or models promoting/encouraging unrealistic body ideals is not going to make your anxiety levels any better, no matter what the context is.

Let's take a look at how social media impacts body image and anxiety by exploring the experience of a friend of mine, who we'll call Emma.

Emma's Struggle with the Flawless Filter Fantasy

At the age of 17, Emma was struggling with moderate acne (which is very common, I might add!). Her anxiety about her skin was mild at first but began to intensify as she spent more time on social media, constantly comparing herself to influencers and peers with flawless, edited skin. These comparisons made her feel rubbish, resulting in a fixation on her appearance. She became convinced that everyone around her was silently judging her and the slightest reference to her skin would trigger feelings of shame and sadness. The anxiety grew with every scroll on social media, to the point where she began cancelling plans with friends and avoiding social events. She truly believed she couldn't compare to the unrealistic standards she saw online.

Over time, and with the help of her amazing support network, Emma realised that her constant comparison to airbrushed people online was harming her mental health. She decided to follow body-positive accounts and limit her time on social media. By doing so, she noticed that her anxiety about her skin began to reduce. She was no longer being exposed to unrealistic standards and instead started to focus on other, more important things. In the process, she became more accepting of herself and gradually re-engaged in meaningful activities.

PRO TIP: Click that unfollow button and switch to following positive content, i.e. accounts that leave you feeling happy, content, good about yourself. You know those pages that are actually going to leave you better off than when you found them. There's an abundance of choice – from educational pages about business and productivity, to self-care accounts (see the chapter Resources and Further Reading for examples). By filling your brain with wholesome content on a regular basis, you're more likely to help those anxious thoughts dissipate right before your eyes.

Strategies for Managing Phone Use

1. Set time for no phone use in the day (e.g. between 9 and 12, 1 and 4, etc.)
2. Set a 'no phone two hours before bed' rule to limit the effect of blue light
3. Leave phone outside room on charge (also helps sleep!)
4. Start/continue a new activity to distract from mobile phone usage
5. Reduce the notifications on certain apps to reduce engagement with/ attraction to apps
6. Set a screen cap on your phone (once one hour on social media is reached, phone alerts you to take time out)
7. Ask your friends/family not to message you after a certain time (e.g. 9pm) unless there is a real emergency (a wardrobe malfunction doesn't count!)

Who knew that stuff like what I eat and how much I move affects my anxiety? Not me. It's reassuring to know that some simple swaps can actually put the brakes on my anxious brain. Maybe all the hoo haa about "small changes make a big difference" isn't just talk after all...'

Me

Reflect & Act: Reset Rituals

Reflect:
- Which of your daily habits (sleep, food, exercise, screen time) might be affecting your mood and anxiety levels the most?

Act:
- Choose one small habit to improve this week (e.g. switching off your phone earlier in the evening or drinking more water).

Supplement your experience via the worksheet in Appendix B of the Additional Resources.

Key Takeaways

Before we move on, here's what to remember from this chapter:

- Diet, exercise, sleep and screen use all impact anxiety levels. Attending to just one in isolation may not help those with significant anxiety, but a combination is likely to lead to an improvement.
- Foods like fatty fish, dark chocolate and fruit can regulate cortisol levels, which helps to reduce stress levels.
- Drinking 1.5 litres of water per day is key to maintaining hydration, which can help manage stress levels.
- Caffeine indirectly activates the release of chemicals and stress hormones into the bloodstream, which can worsen overall feelings of stress.
- Exercise is a natural way of raising endorphin levels and reducing the likelihood of stress.
- Regular exercise helps lower resting cortisol levels over time, helping us to manage stress better.

- Lack of sleep messes with our brain's mood chemicals, throwing our emotions out of whack and leaving us feeling jumbled.
- Prioritising quality sleep and maintaining a stable circadian rhythm is crucial for our mood and overall wellbeing
- We need different amounts of sleep depending on our age to stay balanced—what works for adults might not be enough for teenagers!
- Excessive screen use, particularly before bed, can interfere with the production of melatonin (the hormone that regulates sleep) and increase exposure to stress-inducing content, both of which can cause anxiety levels to rise.

Mission accomplished: Essential Habits Mastered!

Next stop: Now that we've explored how small lifestyle changes- like upgrading our diet, exercise, sleep and reducing our screen use- can help manage anxiety, it's time to go up a gear. It's time to turn our attention to the world of mindfulness and compassion. You'll be provided with some secret gems which can complement and amplify the benefits of your new habits. Ready to learn how mindfulness can change your outlook and help you become the master of your anxiety? Let's get going then!

Notes

1 Eating such foods will not automatically make you feel less stressed, for instance if your sleep pattern is disturbed.
2 You might be wondering why I mentioned that dark chocolate, rather than milk chocolate, helps reduce stress. This is because dark chocolate contains a higher percentage of cocoa, which is high in flavonoids and contains antioxidant properties that help reduce stress.

References

Ali, A. H., Ahmed, H. S., Jawad, A. S. & Mustafa, M. A. (2021). Endorphin: Function and mechanism of action. *Sci Arch, 2*(1), 9–13.

American Psychiatric Association. (2013). *Diagnostic and statistical manual of mental disorders: DSM-5*. American Psychiatric Association.

Baranwal, N., Phoebe, K. Y. & Siegel, N. S. (2023). Sleep physiology, pathophysiology, and sleep hygiene. *Progress in Cardiovascular Diseases, 77*, 59–69.

Barber, T. M. & Sattar, N. (2021). The role of diet in brain health: A focus on vascular function. *Journal of Neuroendocrinology, 33*(1), e12872. https://doi.org/10.1111/jne.12872.

Beaudoin, L. P. (2014). A design-based approach to sleep-onset and insomnia: Super-somnolent mentation, the cognitive shuffle and serial diverse imagining. In *Computational modeling of cognition-emotion interactions: Relevance to mechanisms of affective disorders and therapeutic action* (pp. 147–163). IOS Press.

Blumfield, M., Mayr, H., De Vlieger, N., Abbott, K., Starck, C., Fayet-Moore, F. & Marshall, S. (2022). Should we 'eat a rainbow'? An umbrella review of the health effects of colorful bioactive pigments in fruits and vegetables. *Molecules, 27*(13), 4061.

Castro-Alija, M. J., Albertos, I., Pérez Íñigo, C., López, M., Jiménez, J. M., Cao, M. J., Trayling, M. & Ruiz-Tovar, J. (2023). Association between anxiety status and hydration status in Spanish university students. *Nutrients, 16*(1), 118.

Cay, M., Ucar, C., Senol, D., Çevirgen, F., Ozbag, D., Altay, Z. & Yildiz, S. (2018). Effect of increase in cortisol level due to stress in healthy young individuals on dynamic and static balance scores. *Northern Clinics of Istanbul, 5*(4), 295.

Chellappa, S. L. & Aeschbach, D. (2022). Sleep and anxiety: From mechanisms to interventions. *Sleep Medicine Reviews, 61*, 101583.

D'Angelo, M. & Steardo, L., Jr. (2024). Cannabinoids and sleep: Exploring biological mechanisms and therapeutic potentials. *International Journal of Molecular Sciences, 25*(7), 3603.

Deis, L., Quiroga, A. M. & De Rosas, M. I. (2021). Coloured compounds in fruits and vegetables and health. *Psychiatry and Neuroscience Update: From Epistemology to Clinical Psychiatry, 4*, 343–358. Springer Nature. https://doi.org/10.1007/978-3-030-61721-9_25.

Desai, D., Momin, A., Hirpara, P., Jha, H., Thaker, R. & Patel, J. (2024). Exploring the role of circadian rhythms in sleep and recovery: A review article. *Cureus, 16*(6), e61568.

Ekman, P. & Davidson, R. J. (1993). Voluntary smiling changes regional brain activity. *Psychological Science, 4*(5), 342–345.

Elhai, J. D., Dvorak, R. D., Levine, J. C. & Hall, B. J. (2017). Problematic smartphone use: A conceptual overview and systematic review of relations with anxiety and depression psychopathology. *Psychiatry Research, 248*, 1–13. https://doi.org/10.1016/j.psychres.2016.12.004.

Fazal, M., Irshad, A., Maryam, A., Ashraf, M., Qureshi, M. A. & Khan, R. (2024). Tracking screen time among students during Covid-19 and its association with eye strain, headache & sleep disturbances. *Pakistan Journal of Public Health, 14*(2), 64–69.

Foster, R. (2022). *Life time: The new science of the body clock, and how it can revolutionize your sleep and health*. Penguin.

García, L. C. & Hernández, A. N. M. (2020). Beneficial effects of cocoa and dark chocolate polyphenols on health. *The FASEB Journal, 34*(S1), 1.

Gardiner, C., Weakley, J., Burke, L. M., Roach, G. D., Sargent, C., Maniar, N., Huynh, M., Miller, D. J., Townshend, A. & Halson, S. L. (2024). The effect of alcohol on subsequent sleep in healthy adults: A systematic review and meta-analysis. *Sleep Medicine Reviews, 80*, 102030.

Grant, S. S., Kim, K. & Friedman, B. H. (2023). How long is long enough? Controlling for acute caffeine intake in cardiovascular research. *Brain Sciences, 13*(2), 224.

Grisel, J. E., Bartels, J. L., Allen, S. A. & Turgeon, V. L. (2008). Influence of β-endorphin on anxious behavior in mice: Interaction with EtOH. *Psychopharmacology, 200,* 105–115.

Groeger, J. A., Lo, J. C., Santhi, N., Lazar, A. S. & Dijk, D. J. (2022). Contrasting effects of sleep restriction, total sleep deprivation, and sleep timing on positive and negative affect. *Frontiers in Behavioral Neuroscience, 16,* 911994.

Guest, N. S., VanDusseldorp, T. A., Nelson, M. T., Grgic, J., Schoenfeld, B. J., Jenkins, N. D., Arent, S. M., Antonio, J., Stout, J. R., Trexler, E. T., Smith-Ryan, A. E., Goldstein, E. R., Kalman, D. S. & Campbell, B. I. (2021). International society of sports nutrition position stand: Caffeine and exercise performance. *Journal of the International Society of Sports Nutrition, 18*(1), 1.

Hsu, M. F., Raub, B., Forman, D. E. & Calfas, K. J. (January, 2017). Just 20 minutes of exercise decreases inflammatory responses: A study on moderate exercise and inflammation. *Brain, Behavior, and Immunity, 64,* 252–260. https://doi.org/10.1016/j.bbi.2017.01.009.

Hunter, W. (2024, November 28). The exact amount of time the average Briton spends scrolling on their smartphone each day—with Gen Z women clocking up the most hours. *The Telegraph.*

Kaida, K., Mori, I., Kihara, K. & Kaida, N. (2023). The function of REM and NREM sleep on memory distortion and consolidation. *Neurobiology of Learning and Memory, 204,* 107811.

Klumpers, U. M., Veltman, D. J., van Tol, M. J., Kloet, R. W., Boellaard, R., Lammertsma, A. A. & Hoogendijk, W. J. (2015). Neurophysiological effects of sleep deprivation in healthy adults, a pilot study. *PloS One, 10*(1), e0116906.

Lane, M. M., Gamage, E., Travica, N., Dissanayaka, T., Ashtree, D. N., Gauci, S., Lotfaliany, M., O'Neil, A., Jacka, Felice N. & Marx, W. (2022). Ultra-processed food consumption and mental health: A systematic review and meta-analysis of observational studies. *Nutrients, 14*(13), 2568. https://doi.org/10.3390/nu14132568.

Moosavi-Movahedi, A. A., Moosavi-Movahedi, F. & Yousefi, R. (2021). Good sleep as an important pillar for a healthy life. In A. A. Moosavi-Movahedi (Ed.), *Rationality and scientific lifestyle for health* (pp. 167–195). Springer. https://doi.org/10.1007/978-3-030-74326-0_10.

NHS. (2021). *Physical activity guidelines for adults aged 19 to 64.* https://www.nhs.uk/live-well/exercise/.

Nobari, H., Banihashemi, M., Saedmocheshi, S., Prieto-González, P. & Oliveira, R. (2023). Overview of the impact of sleep monitoring on optimal performance, immune system function and injury risk reduction in athletes: A narrative review. *Science progress, 106*(4), 00368504231206265.

Oros-Peusquens, A. M., Loução, R., Abbas, Z., Gras, V., Zimmermann, M. & Shah, N. J. (2019). A single-scan, rapid whole-brain protocol for quantitative water content mapping with neurobiological implications. *Frontiers in Neurology, 10,* 1333. https://doi.org/10.3389/fneur.2019.01333.

Park, S., Kang, I., Edden, R. A., Namgung, E., Kim, J. & Kim, J. (2020). Shorter sleep duration is associated with lower GABA levels in the anterior cingulate cortex. *Sleep Medicine, 71,* 1–7.

Portas, C. M., Bjorvatn, B. & Ursin, R. (2000). Serotonin and the sleep/wake cycle: Special emphasis on microdialysis studies. *Progress in Neurobiology, 60*(1), 13–35.

Public Health England. (2016). *The Eatwell Guide.* https://www.gov.uk/government/publications/the-eatwell-guide.

Rodak, K., Kokot, I. & Kratz, E. M. (2021). Caffeine as a factor influencing the functioning of the human body—friend or foe? *Nutrients, 13*(9), 3088.

Rosa-Neto, J. C., Lira, F. S., Little, J. P., Landells, G., Islam, H., Chazaud, B., Pyne, D. B., Teixeira, A. M., Batatinha, H., Antunes, B. M., Minuzzi, L. G., Palmowksi, J., Simpson, R. J. & Krüger, K. (2022). Immunometabolism-fit: How exercise and training can modify T cell and macrophage metabolism in health and disease. *Exercise Immunology Review, 28*, 29–46.

Ruiz-Tejada, A., Neisewander, J. & Katsanos, C. S. (2022). Regulation of voluntary physical activity behavior: A review of evidence involving dopaminergic pathways in the brain. *Brain Sciences, 12*(3), 333.

Sabaei, Y., Sarshin, A., Rahimi, A. & Feizolahi, F. (2022). The effect of caffeine supplementation and exhausting exercise on inflammatory factors in hot environments. *Razi Journal of Medical Sciences, 29*(10), 211–221.

Sharma, V. K., Sharma, A., Verma, K. K., Gaur, P. K., Kaushik, R. & Abdali, B. (2023). A comprehensive review on pharmacological potentials of caffeine. *Journal of Applied Pharmaceutical Sciences and Research, 6*(3), 16–26.

Silvani, M. I., Werder, R. & Perret, C. (2022). The influence of blue light on sleep, performance and wellbeing in young adults: A systematic review. *Frontiers in Physiology, 13*, 943108.

Solomou, S., Logue, J., Reilly, S. & Perez-Algorta, G. (2023). A systematic review of the association of diet quality with the mental health of university students: Implications in health education practice. *Health Education Research, 38*(1), 28–68.

Stanhope, K. L. (2016). Sugar consumption, metabolic disease, and obesity: The state of the controversy. *The American Journal of Clinical Nutrition, 103*(1), 1–10.

Tang, H. Y., Jiang, A. J., Wang, X. Y., Wang, H., Guan, Y. Y., Li, F. & Shen, G. M. (2021). Uncovering the pathophysiology of irritable bowel syndrome by exploring the gut-brain axis: A narrative review. *Annals of Translational Medicine, 9*(14).

Urizar, G. G., Miller, K., Saldaña, K. S., Garovoy, N., Sweet, C. M. C. & King, A. C. (2021). Effects of health behavior interventions on psychosocial outcomes and cortisol regulation among chronically stressed midlife and older adults. *International Journal of Behavioral Medicine, 28*(5), 627–640. https://doi.org/10.1007/s12529-021-09957-1.

van Zonneveld, S. M., van den Oever, E. J., Haarman, B. C., Grandjean, E. L., Nuninga, J. O., van de Rest, O. & Sommer, I. E. (2024). An anti-inflammatory diet and its potential benefit for individuals with mental disorders and neurodegenerative diseases—A narrative review. *Nutrients, 16*(16), 2646.

Varanoske, A. N., McClung, H. L., Sepowitz, J. J., Halagarda, C. J., Farina, E. K., Berryman, C. E., Lieberman, H. R., McClung, J. P., Pasiakos, S. M. & Karl, J. P. (2022). Stress and the gut-brain axis: Cognitive performance, mood state, and biomarkers of blood-brain barrier and intestinal permeability following severe physical and psychological stress. *Brain, Behavior, and Immunity, 101*, 383–393.

Werner-Gray, L. (2020). *Anxiety-free with food: Natural, science-backed strategies to relieve stress and support your mental health*. Hay House, Inc.

Wirtz, P. H., von Känel, R., Meister, R. E., Arpagaus, A., Treichler, S., Kuebler, U., Huber, S. & Ehlert, U. (2014). Dark chocolate intake buffers stress reactivity in humans. *Journal of the American College of Cardiology, 63*(21), 2297–2299.

Wright, K. P., Jr, Drake, A. L., Frey, D. J., Fleshner, M., Desouza, C. A., Gronfier, C. & Czeisler, C. A. (2015). Influence of sleep deprivation and circadian misalignment on cortisol, inflammatory markers, and cytokine balance. *Brain, Behavior, and Immunity, 47*, 24–34.

Yegane, Z. A., Nasiri, A., Sahranavard, S. & Sebzari, A. R. (2024). Effect of online mindfulness-based stress reduction intervention on sleep quality of breast cancer patients. *Modern Care Journal, 21*(1).

Yin, J., Julius, A. A. & Wen, J. T. (2021). Optimization of light exposure and sleep schedule for circadian rhythm entrainment. *Plos one, 16*(6), e0251478.

Zaplatosch, M. E. & Adams, W. M. (2020). The effect of acute hypohydration on indicators of glycemic regulation, appetite, metabolism and stress: A systematic review and meta-analysis. *Nutrients, 12*(9), 2526.

Zheng, R. (2022). Pleasure and achievement: Dopamine and endorphins. *Highlights in Science, Engineering and Technology, 6*, 83–89.

7 Keep Calm and Mindfully On
Finding Your Zen

> I tried it the other day-
>   just for a few minutes-
> and something changed.
>   My mind felt clearer-

Figure 7.1 A glimpse into my thoughts: a page from my personal journal.

Spiritual teacher and author, Eckhart Tolle, argues that all of our anxious states stem from a tendency to focus too much on the future and not enough on the present.

> **GOAL:** To explore self-compassion and simple mindfulness techniques, and why these practices are effective tools for managing stress.

7.1 Understanding and Practising Compassion

Our brains have evolved over many millions of years making them very complex. This is why our emotions can be difficult to understand and regulate as we are relying on the survival instincts that our 'old brains' had. In prehistoric times, when humans were faced with threats to life—like a lion—our muscles tensed, breathing quickened and heart rate quickened. These reactions to stressful encounters, a.k.a. the 'fight or flight' response,

DOI: 10.4324/9781003670117-8

help our old brains react promptly to life-threating situations to keep us safe/ protect us.

According to Compassion Focused Therapy (CFT), we have three 'systems' that regulate our emotions and responses (Lopes & Silva, 2020).

- **Threat system:** helps us detect and respond to potential dangers. It initiates feelings such as anger and shame.
- **Drive system:** motivates us to pursue goals and rewards. This system is associated with feelings of excitement and achievement.
- **Soothing system:** designed to balance the threat and drive systems, helping to find calm, safety and compassion.

CFT aims to activate the soothing system, which helps us feel safe, content, and calm. It also encourages us to be kinder to ourselves. By understanding ourselves a little better, we can be more compassionate to ourselves and others.

Take a look at Figure 7.2. to see how the different systems interact:

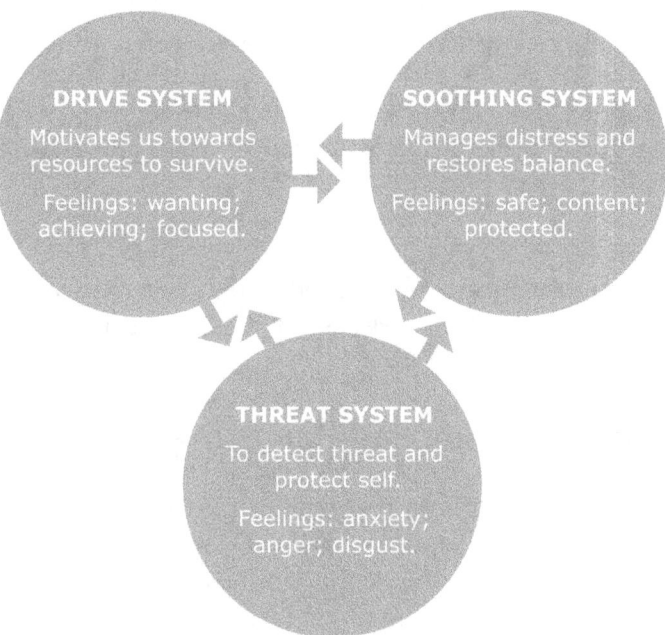

Figure 7.2 A diagram illustrating the three-part emotion regulation system: Drive, Soothing and Threat.

How Does CFT Work in Practice?

During a therapy session, clients learn to identify when their threat system is activated (e.g. when they experience muscle tension, racing heart, etc.) and learn that this is not a sign of real danger, but rather the body's natural alarm system going off.

CFT focuses on engaging the soothing system through practising self-compassion. For example, repeating to yourself: 'It's okay to feel over-whelmed right now—I'm doing my best and that's more than anyone can ask. Most importantly—I'm safe and I can handle what comes my way.'

This is when clients may be suggested to try out some breathing and visualisation exercises (see later in chapter), which can help trigger the soothing system, reducing their heart rate and calming down the nervous system.

CFT also looks at balancing the drive system, to foster motivation and the pursuit of meaningful goals, without the presence of an overly harsh self-critic. It does so by replacing negative thoughts like 'I am never going to be able to do this' with positive ones to promote kindness and contentment.

If, for example, a client had to deliver a presentation, they might be advised to:

- Take a few deep, slow breaths before going into the room where they are to present, to help engage their soothing system.
- Notice when their anxious thoughts crop up, sit with them, and treat themselves with kindness rather than letting their self-critic run the show.
- Remind themselves of what they have achieved and how far they've come. Revisit the evidence and significance of their prior successes and strengths, to initiate the drive system in a calm and balanced way.
- Reflect regularly with compassion, ensuring they appreciate the courage it took to face the situation as opposed to shining a light on the perceived mistakes.

Through CFT, clients learn to move from an overly reactive fight or flight response to a more balanced and calm state, where the three systems are working together, governed by the soothing system. This can help to dampen the intensity of different types of stress—whether it be workplace, social, academic, financial—and protect mental wellbeing as time passes.

It's all well and good telling people to be more compassionate to themselves but is there actually any evidence that proves it helps?

The answer is yes! Research has shown an association between compassion-related practices and improved anxiety.

Here is an example:

Wilson et al. (2019) looked at 22 randomised controlled trials (RCTs)* and concluded that therapies focusing on self-compassion, including compassion-focused therapy, mindfulness-based cognitive therapy and acceptance and commitment therapy, were effective in decreasing symptoms of anxiety and depression.

In fact, research has repeatedly shown that individuals who are more kind and understanding towards themselves tend to experience lower levels of anxiety. For example, Neff and Germer (2012) found that participants who underwent an eight-week Mindful Self-Compassion programme showed a significant reduction in anxiety levels.

*An RCT is considered the 'gold standard' of scientific experimentation. Participants are randomly assigned to an experimental group (a new intervention or treatment) or a control group (a standard treatment, a placebo, or no treatment at all, depending on the study). This method allows experimenters to determine whether the observed differences between the groups are due to the intervention itself or to other factors.

PRO TIP: Create a 'Mindfulness Jar'—a tangible reminder of the daily moments of peace and joy to help cultivate a positive mindset.
- Step 1: Find a small jar or container that you like.
- Step 2: Personalise it with your favourite colours, stickers or doodles that bring you joy, or you find comforting.
- Step 3: Each day, on a small piece of paper, write down a positive moment, a feeling of calm or serenity, or even an achievement.
- Step 4: At the end of the week, read them back to remind yourself of the positive moments you've experienced. We all need a reminder of the good things in life sometimes!

Meditation is to the mind what exercise is to the body—it warms and invigorates.

John Thornton, merchant and philanthropist

So, How Can I Practise Being Compassionate To Myself?

There are many ways to practise self-compassion, and we'll go through a few of these in this book. Firstly, breathing exercises help activate the soothing system and can be useful in times of distress. When we breathe, we inhale oxygen, which is used by the body. This creates carbon dioxide which we exhale as a waste product. When our breathing is relaxed, our levels of oxygen and carbon dioxide are balanced, allowing our body to function effectively. It's unsurprising that we are advised to take deep breaths when we are about to do something nerve-racking, like an interview or presentation. Before every single interview I've done, my dad has always said to me, *'Stop. Take three slow, deep breaths—in and out. Smile. You've got this!'* Granted, it sounds like something Sharpay Evans would say, with a side of jazz hands, but if it works, who am I to undermine her practices! (That was a *High School Musical* reference—for those of you who somehow bypassed peak British teen culture!)

Anyway, where were we? Breathing exercises can be done in several minutes, making them easy to administer in just about any circumstance with the smallest time window.

Leyro et al. (2021) conducted a meta-analysis of 40 RCTs examining anxiety treatments. They found that the treatments comprising a respiratory component (i.e. focused on breathing) showed greater improvements in anxiety levels compared with the control group (receiving treatment with no respiratory component).

To make it a bit easier, I have chosen some mindfulness exercises, each differing in length, for you to try! Research has demonstrated the effectiveness of all these exercises.

Supplement your experience via the worksheet in Appendix C of the Additional Resources.

7.2 Mindfulness Exercises

Model Hailey Bieber has spoken openly about how meditation and therapy have been influential in her life. She strongly advocates for these strategies as her first port of call when facing challenges.

Breathing Exercises

Belly Breathing (10–20 minutes)

This is formally known as diaphragmatic breathing (the diaphragm is a muscle in your belly). By practising belly breathing, you can train your body to breathe more productively by opening up your lungs. This is because breathing into our belly demonstrates that you are breathing using your diaphragm which confirms you are using the bottom of your lungs, increasing oxygen in the blood and using less energy per breath.

Benefits:

- Reduces anxiety
- Promotes relaxation
- Improves flow of oxygen to the brain and body

Ma et al. (2017) conducted a study to investigate the effects of diaphragmatic breathing. Forty healthy participants were assigned to either a breathing intervention group (BIG) or a control group (no intervention). They found that those in the BIG group had significantly lower cortisol levels after training, whilst the control group showed no significant change in cortisol levels.

> Dr Russ Harris, author of The Happiness Trap, advocates for the power of slow breathing—likening it to an anchor, helping keep you grounded until the storm passes.

Follow these steps to try it out for yourself:

- Step 1: Find a comfortable, quiet room and lie on your back with your knees bent (you can also do this exercise sitting upright on a chair if you prefer).
- Step 2: Put one hand on your chest and the other on your stomach.
- Step 3: Breathe in slowly through your nose until you can't take in any more air. Feel the air move through your body.
- Step 3: Breathe out slowly through pursed lips (imagine you are sipping through a straw).
- Step 4: Repeat the above steps a few times for best results.

Let's look at how someone might use belly breathing to help manage anxiety in a relatable, real-life context:

Sami's Breathing Tale

Sami was waiting patiently outside the exam hall, about to go in for her first university history exam. Her chest felt tight, and her hands were clammy. She had been revising for weeks on end, and now it had finally arrived. All she could think was, 'I can't remember anything I've learnt. I'm going to have nothing to write. Help.'

She remembered a technique her mum taught her after she'd been to a therapist, called belly breathing. It was quick and simple—perfect for the five minutes she had spare before she'd be ushered into the room of torment. She found a quiet space round the corner of the exam hall. She sat upright and placed one hand on her chest and the other on her stomach. She closed her eyes and breathed slowly through her nose, vaguely aware of the hand on her stomach slowly rising and falling. She slowly counted in her head as she breathed in. After pausing briefly, she exhaled in the same slow and controlled manner.

After a few repetitions, she noticed her heart rate had slowed down dramatically, and her mind seemed to have calmed some-what. After a few minutes, she felt ready. Whilst the anxiety hadn't dissipated completely, she felt more anchored. It was okay to be anxious; she could control it. She walked into the exam hall like she was born for it!

The Signal Breath (5 minutes)

This is a stress reduction technique which helps you to reset during times of stress by taking time to focus on your breath.

Benefits:
- Provides a quick reset during moments of stress
- Increases self-awareness
- Facilitates relaxation

Follow these steps to try it out for yourself:

- Step 1: Take a deep breath.
- Step 2: Now, let it go and say 'calm' to yourself.
- Step 3: Tighten your shoulders and arms; hold it for a few seconds.
- Step 4: Allow your jaw, shoulders and arms to go loose and limp.

You know how I always used to poo-poo breathing exercises...
thinking they were a bit "wishy-washy", well I've done a 180! I tried
it the other day—just for a few minutes—and something changed.
My mind felt clearer. I felt calm, as opposed to the usual chaos
happening internally and externally (you know better than anyone!).
Who knew something so simple could be so powerful?

Me

Compassionate Colour Breathing

This exercise is partly inspired by Compassionate Breathing with Visualisation, a technique used in Compassionate Mind Training, developed by Professor Paul Gilbert. It helps anchor the mind and body in compassion through engaging the imagination.

Benefits:

- Builds warmth and kindness
- Reduces self-criticism
- Improves emotional regulation

Follow these steps to try it out for yourself:

- Step 1: Make sure you're sitting comfortably. Start by slowing your breathing to a comfortable rhythm—about five breaths per minute.
- Step 2: On the inhale, imagine breathing in warmth, compassion and a calming colour (e.g. blue or lilac).
- Step 3: Exhale slowly while imagining breathing out a colour that represents stress (e.g. black or red) whilst you send warmth to areas of tension in your body.
- Step 4: Repeat this 3–5 times.

Optional: If it feels helpful, try pairing this with phrases like *'May I be grounded', 'May I meet myself with compassion and understanding', 'May I find strength to keep pushing forward'.*

Research shows that the combination of breathwork and visualisation can reduce anxiety and self-criticism by calming the nervous system. For instance, Rockliff et al. (2008) found that when people practised calm breathwork while visualising compassion—such as imagining warmth or light—their heart rate variability (HRV) increased, a marker of calming nervous system activity.

Guided Imagery Exercises

Guided imagery is a technique involving using mental images to induce feelings of safety and calm—for example, imagining yourself in a serene and peaceful place like a quiet beach. It can be used to reduce stress and promote healing. Researchers have found many benefits of practising this exercise on stress levels. Let's take a look at some of these.

- Beizaee et al. (2018) conducted an RCT to explore the effects of guided imagery on anxiety and depression in patients on hemodialysis (a treatment used for people with chronic renal failure). Eighty participants undergoing treatment were randomly assigned to the guided imagery (intervention) group or the control group (no intervention/ routine care). Anxiety levels were significantly lower in the intervention group.
- Alam et al. (2016) conducted an RCT to assess the effects of recorded guided imagery during surgical procedures. They found that the anxiety of surgeons significantly reduced when listening to guided imagery recordings.
- Beck, Hansen and Gold (2015) conducted a study to investigate the effects of guided imagery techniques on work-related anxiety. They divided 20 participants into two groups; one group was given a nine-week guided imagery and music programme whilst the other group received no treatment. The guided imagery & music group showed significant improvements in wellbeing and stress management compared with the no-treatment group. The guided imagery and music group also showed greater reduction in cortisol levels (as we learnt earlier, this is the body's main stress hormone).

Short Body Scan (5–10 minutes)

In this technique you are guided to focus on different parts of your body, helping you develop a stronger awareness of your physical sensations, which can promote relaxation and reduce anxiety. The key to body scan meditation is to observe without judgement.

- Step 1: Find a quiet space where you can lie down comfortably, either on a yoga mat or your bed.
- Step 2: Close your eyes and bring your awareness to your body. Start with your toes and gradually move your attention up through each part of your body, through your legs, bum, lower back, etc. Notice any sensations without judgement.
- Step 3: Spend a few breaths on each area, gently releasing tension and allowing yourself to relax deeper into the ground.
- Step 4: Complete the body scan from head to toe. Feel a sense of relaxation and presence throughout your entire body.

Have no time but need to release some tension? Try this 60-second body scan:

- Step 1: Tense your shoulders for five seconds.
- Step 2: Slowly exhale and relax your shoulders.
- Step 3: Tense your fists for five seconds.
- Step 4: Slowly exhale and relax your fists.

Continue with different muscle groups to help you release built-up tension and calm your mind.

The Perfect Day Exercise (10–30 minutes)

Endorsed by renowned neuroscientists Dr Andrew Huberman and Dr Martha Beck, this visualisation technique is designed to help optimise well-being and productivity by clarifying priorities and taking meaningful action to live intentionally.

Follow these steps to try it out for yourself:

- Step 1: Find a quiet space, free from distractions (yes, that means putting your phone aside for a few minutes!). Get a pen and some paper.
- Step 2: Write down what your perfect day looks like, from morning through to night. Be clear and detailed—what time did you wake up,

where and with whom? Describe your morning, afternoon and evening routines. Be specific, as if someone were to relive the day using only your description as guidance.

- Step 3: Review what you've written. How does this day align with your current life? What changes can you make today to bring elements of your perfect day into reality?
- Step 4: Identify the small steps that can help move you closer to this. Jot them down. Follow them. Stick with them.

Meadow Meditation (10–20 minutes)

This visualisation technique guides individuals to explore the sights, sounds and sensations of a meadow. Immersing oneself in the serene imagery of a meadow helps cultivate a greater sense of awareness and inner peace, leading to a reduction in stress and anxiety.

Follow these steps to try it out for yourself:

Close your eyes and take a few deep breaths, allowing yourself to relax and let go of any tension in your body. As you continue to breathe deeply, imagine yourself in a serene meadow surrounded by lush green grass, colourful wildflowers, and tall trees swaying gently in the breeze. In the distance, you can hear the gentle babbling of a stream, inviting you to explore its tranquil waters.

- Step 1: Visualising the meadow:
  - Picture yourself standing in the middle of the meadow, feeling the soft grass beneath your feet and the warm sunlight kissing your skin.
  - Take a moment to observe your surroundings, noticing the vibrant colours of the flowers, the gentle rustling of the leaves and the clear blue sky above.
  - Allow yourself to be fully immersed in the beauty and serenity of the meadow, feeling a sense of peace and tranquillity wash over you.
- Step 2: Approaching the stream:
  - As you take a step forward, you find yourself walking towards the source of the soothing sound—the gentle stream that winds its way through the meadow.

- Follow the path of the stream, feeling the cool breeze and the refreshing mist of water as you draw nearer to its banks.
- Notice how the sunlight dances on the surface of the stream, creating shimmering patterns of light and shadow.
- Step 3: Sitting by the stream:
  - Find a comfortable spot by the edge of the stream and take a seat, allowing yourself to fully connect with the natural world around you.
  - Close your eyes and listen to the rhythmic flow of the water, feeling a deep sense of relaxation and contentment with each breath you take.
  - Allow any thoughts or worries to gently drift away, leaving you feeling grounded and at peace in this tranquil oasis.
- Step 4: Exploring the stream:
  - If you feel inclined, dip your toes into the cool, crystal-clear water of the stream, feeling its refreshing touch against your skin.
  - Take a moment to explore the stream's surroundings, noticing the smooth stones lining its bed, the graceful movements of fish swimming beneath the surface and the delicate ripples created by your presence.
- Step 5: Closing:
  - When you're ready, take a few deep breaths and slowly open your eyes, bringing your awareness back to the present moment.
  - Carry the sense of peace and tranquillity you experienced in the meadow and stream with you as you go about your day, knowing that you can return to this serene oasis in your mind whenever you need a moment of calm and relaxation.

Take your time to savour this tranquil experience, fully immersing yourself in the sights, sounds, and sensations of the meadow and stream.

Progress comes with practice. It takes time. Keep showing up.

Model Kendall Jenner once described having a panic attack whilst flying—her heart was racing, and she felt numb. She later realised how much power the mind has and how deeply her anxiety was rooted there. She explained that what helps her now is redirecting her focus, using techniques like grounding to bring herself back to the present.

7.3 Grounding Techniques

Grounding techniques are a form of mindfulness. Sometimes anxious thoughts can feel very overwhelming. It may be helpful to try distracting yourself by re-focusing on the present. Grounding is a practical way of calming anxiety by isolating the senses. The concept of grounding was coined by Lowen (1993), a psychotherapist.

Why not try some and see what you think!

The 5-4-3-2-1 Method

This is a very popular technique. List things you notice around you using your senses, starting at five and working backwards. For example:

- Step 1: five things you hear
- Step 2: four things you see
- Step 3: three things you can touch from where you're sitting
- Step 4: two things you can smell
- Step 5: one thing you can taste

Shift Your Attention

This is similar to the 5-4-3-2-1 exercise above but now the focus is on something specific, which helps distract the brain from the anxiety taking over.

How does it work?

1. Firstly, become aware of what it is that is causing the distress. It may be a thought, a physical sensation or an event.
2. Pause and acknowledge how you are feeling. Recognise that these feelings of anxiety are temporary, and that you can manage them.
3. Shift your attention from the trigger onto something else. This could be anything that engages your senses (in a positive way).

For example:

- Focus on your breathing by paying attention to the rise and fall of your chest.
- Observe what's around you: what can you see, hear, smell, taste or touch? Describe these sensory experiences in detail to yourself.
- Repeat positive affirmations to yourself such as 'I can handle this'.
- Count something to help redirect your focus, such as counting all the red things you can see in the room.

Esther's Blind Panic

I was at a concert with my cousin, about to see the man himself—Robbie Williams. As the music started building, ready for his big entrance, her vision suddenly went. 'Oh god—I can't see,' she exclaimed repeatedly, her heart pounding at a million miles an hour. I could tell she was beginning to panic. I knew she'd had panic attacks before, so I was fairly sure this was another one. But the fear she was feeling was intense—distressing for her and for us watching. I gently led her out of the crowd, and we sat down against a pillar. She kept saying she couldn't see and was breathing very fast. 'I'm here. I'm not going anywhere,' I told her. 'Breathe in for two seconds... and out for two seconds,' I said softly, matching my breath to hers. As her breathing slowed a little, I asked her to notice what she could feel around her—her feet on the ground, the pillar against her back, the feel of my hands in hers. I asked her if she could hear the rhythm of the music playing, the sounds of voices muttering. She nodded several times as she continued taking slow, steady breaths. Little by little, I started to notice her focus shifting from the overwhelming fear inside to the simple, steady sensations around her. The panic didn't disappear instantly, but grounding herself in the present helped her feel a bit steadier and in control.

The key with grounding techniques is to keep practising as regularly as possible. They need to become part of your standard daily routine. Early intervention has been seen to offer both short- and long-term relief. Research has shown that intervening early can catch symptoms in their tracks before they escalate as well as being effective in producing a long-term reduction in anxiety problems.

If You Need More Support

If you notice your symptoms getting out of hand, or you feel some guidance might be necessary, it is okay to seek support from a professional.* Therapy, whether on a 1:1 or group basis, can equip you with the necessary tools to reduce the prevalence and magnitude of your symptoms and improve wellbeing.

It is important to seek professional help if your anxiety is persistent and/or debilitating. Doctors and health professionals are there to help—they can provide support and signpost you to appropriate treatments (like talking therapies) where needed.

Reflect & Act: Finding Your Zen

Reflect:
- Which CFT 'system' has been in charge lately—the threat, drive or soothing system?

Act:
- Do something intentionally slowly today, like making a cuppa, taking a shower, or walking. Notice each movement. Slowness can signal safety to your nervous system.

Key Takeaways

Before we move on, here's what to remember from this chapter:

- Compassion-Focused Therapy (CFT) suggests that we have three 'systems' that regulate our emotions and responses: the soothing system, the drive system and the threat system.
- There are many quick and simple mindfulness exercises you can put into practice right away, all of which are backed by science.
- You can try some easy breathing exercises like 'Belly Breathing' and 'The Signal Breath'.
- Guided imagery is a useful technique to induce feelings of safety and calm through mental imagery. The 'Short Body Scan' and 'Meadow Meditation' are a good starting point.
- Grounding techniques are a helpful way of distracting yourself from anxious thoughts and re-focusing on the present. The '5-4-3-2-1' method is the most popular, but it may not resonate with you as much as 'Shift Your Attention'. Try both and see what sticks.

Mission accomplished: Finding Calm through Compassion and Breath.

Next stop: We dive into journalling, positive self-talk and setting meaningful goals. You'll also take on an anxiety-busting challenge designed to put your new skills into action—one small step at a time.

References

Alam, M., Roongpisuthipong, W., Kim, N. A., Goyal, A., Swary, J. H., Brindise, R. T., Iyengar, S., Pace, N., West, D. P., Polavarapu, M. & Yoo, S. (2016). Utility of recorded guided imagery and relaxing music in reducing patient pain and anxiety, and surgeon anxiety, during cutaneous surgical procedures: A single-blinded randomized controlled trial. *Journal of the American Academy of Dermatology, 75*(3), 585–589.

Beck, B. D., Hansen, Å. M. & Gold, C. (2015). Coping with work-related stress through guided imagery and music (GIM): Randomized controlled trial. *Journal of Music Therapy, 52*(3), 323–352.

Beizaee, Y., Rejeh, N., Heravi-Karimooi, M., Tadrisi, S. D., Griffiths, P. & Vaismoradi, M. (2018). The effect of guided imagery on anxiety, depression and vital signs in patients on hemodialysis. *Complementary Therapies in Clinical Practice, 33*, 184–190.

Leyro, T. M., Versella, M. V., Yang, M. J., Brinkman, H. R., Hoyt, D. L. & Lehrer, P. (2021). Respiratory therapy for the treatment of anxiety: Meta-analytic review and regression. *Clinical Psychology Review, 84*, 101980.

Lopes, A. F. & Silva, F. M. (2020). Compassion-focused therapy (CFT). In *EFPT psychotherapy guidebook* (2nd ed., p. 11). https://doi.org/10.21428/fc0b32aa.3296abfc.

Lowen, A. (1993). *Depression and the body: The biological basis of faith and reality.* Penguin.

Ma, X., Yue, Z. Q., Gong, Z. Q., Zhang, H., Duan, N. Y., Shi, Y. T., Wei, G. X. & Li, Y. F. (2017). The effect of diaphragmatic breathing on attention, negative affect and stress in healthy adults. *Frontiers in Psychology, 8*, 234806.

Neff, K. D. & Germer, C. K. (2013). A pilot study and randomized controlled trial of the mindful self-compassion program. *Journal of Clinical Psychology, 69*(1), 28–44.

Rockliff, H., Gilbert, P., McEwan, K., Lightman, S. & Glover, D. (2008). A pilot exploration of heart rate variability and salivary cortisol responses to compassion-focused imagery. *Clinical Neuropsychiatry: Journal of Treatment Evaluation. 5*(3), 132–139.

Wilson, A. C., Mackintosh, K., Power, K. & Chan, S. W. (2019). Effectiveness of self-compassion related therapies: A systematic review and meta-analysis. *Mindfulness, 10*, 979–995.

8 Building Your Anxiety Toolkit
Small Shifts for Big Changes

I just need to get it out so it doesn't stay stuck in.

Figure 8.1 A glimpse into my thoughts: a page from my personal journal.

> **GOAL:** Offer daily strategies, including journalling, positive self-talk and goal setting, to effectively manage and reduce stress.

If you hadn't clocked it yet, feeling anxious is pretty common. But here's the good news: there are some practical, daily tips that make managing anxiety a whole lot easier. Learn how documenting your thoughts, positive self-talk and setting achievable goals can fit into your routine. This chapter aims to build on the lifestyle and mindfulness practices you've embraced and provide you with the tools to help you keep on track and live your best, stress-free life. Sound good? Let's dive in and outsmart that anxiety once and for all!

Disclosure: I only promote practices that I personally follow or would recommend to my loved ones, so consider yourself in on something special!

8.1 How Does Writing It Out Relieve Stress?

Writing can be an effective tool for managing anxiety. Journalling is another form of mindfulness, offering a structured way of processing thoughts and

DOI: 10.4324/9781003670117-9

emotions. It allows the mind to slow down and reflect, making it a helpful ally in the pursuit of mental wellbeing.

Young Me's Big Epiphany

In my early teens, I struggled to express my feelings out loud. Couple that with the storm of emotions (associated with puberty, of course), my mood was turbulent to say the least! On one occasion, I recall a friend advising me to write down my feelings when I next felt overwhelmed. My friend told me to write down anything and everything that came into my head, and then to rip the paper up into tiny pieces and throw it in the bin. It seemed bizarre to me at the time, but, after trying it, I experienced an overwhelming sense of catharsis—as if a weight had been lifted off my shoulders. After that, I wrote a lot about my thoughts and feelings. Low and behold, I was unintentionally journalling. This was a form of expression to me. Don't get me wrong, writing about your feelings isn't going to suddenly expel them, but it can help you process and understand them more effectively.

Brain Boost

One study investigated the effect of online Positive Affect Journalling (PAJ) on mental distress. They randomly assigned a group of distressed patients with medical conditions to either a 12-week online PAJ treatment or a control group (usual care). The PAJ group received 15-minute journalling sessions on three days each week. Researchers compared their psychological and physical wellbeing from baseline through to end of treatment. They found that those in the PAJ group had reduced mental distress and increased wellbeing compared to the control group. This provides important insights into the value of journalling for mental wellbeing in medical populations (Smyth et al., 2018).

The best part about journalling? There are no rules! You can write about whatever you want, whenever you want, and however you want. We're not trying to publish a novel here, it's just about 'freeing up' space to offload your thoughts. Write about what is giving you anxiety at the current moment. The stress is often associated with what 'could' happen rather than what 'has' happened. What thoughts and feelings are coming up for you right now? Transferring feelings to paper can be very cathartic.

Try it for yourself: *Start Your Own Journalling Practice*

Step 1. Find yourself a nice notebook (or even just some scraps of paper!).
Step 2. Start writing for five to 15 minutes about whatever comes into your mind. Don't worry about spelling or grammar; that's not important.

It's as simple as that. Try it every day for a week and see what you think!

Journalling can help people express themselves and may help you. However, more serious symptoms may also require professional support. If you revisit your words and find your comments are concerning, please seek professional help (see Resources and Further Reading chapter).

> *Sometimes I just don't know who to turn to, but I just need to get it out so it doesn't stay stuck in. There's just some stuff I'm not ready to say out loud yet. I know you'll just listen. Writing it all down helps me feel lighter, like I've cleared some space in my head again...*
>
> Me

8.2 What Are the Benefits of Positive Self-Talk?

Brené Brown, a writer and research professor, encourages us to treat ourselves with the same kindness and compassion we would offer to someone we love (Brown, 2012). Your thoughts and beliefs about yourself and the world have a huge influence on your life. If you knew the power of these assumptions, you would be pulling out all the stops to change them. Positive self-talk can help you to shift your mindset from negative to positive. The way we talk 'about' ourselves and 'to' ourselves is very important. All too often our inner voice is overly critical and harsh.

The narrative you tell yourself plays a key role in the presentation and continuance of anxiety. We have a tendency as individuals to engage in negative self-talk when something goes wrong or doesn't live up to our pristine standards. Think about a time when something went slightly wrong, or you felt you failed in some way. Now think about how you spoke to yourself in the immediate aftermath: was it positive and supportive, or negative and pessimistic? In most cases, I'm pretty sure negative is the answer. This inner dialogue depletes self-esteem, reinforces negative beliefs about yourself and fuels anxiety. Could you imagine if you spoke to your friends/family/loved ones the way you spoke to yourself in times of crisis? It's likely you wouldn't have any friends anymore. So next time you talk to yourself, make sure the words are compassionate, kind and supportive. As actor Wentworth Miller once said, *'Start the work of being your own best friend.'*

In a world plagued by negativity, both online and offline, if we lead with kindness towards ourselves and others, the world might just become a better place for us all.

PRO TIP: Jake Humphrey, host of the *High Performance* podcast, believes a strong mindset can change the way your life plays out. By consciously training your brain to look for the good, you will start to see more of it. He shared a powerful (and quick!) exercise on his social media recently. He encouraged his followers to create a page on their Notes app called 'Great things are happening to me'. Every day, add one positive thing that happened to you, no matter how small—*'Got a lovely message from my mate Ella today'* or *'Got my list of work tasks ticked off today'.* When you have a bad day, review the list to remind yourself that, even when life looks bleak, good things are happening and you are making progress. There is an important message here—our mindset holds a lot of power. Choose to use it with intention and gratitude, and you're significantly more likely to notice and attract opportunities. Your world is likely to look a whole lot brighter.

In the following story, I'll share with you a challenging period where my own negative thoughts had a significant impact on me during my teenage years.

From Track Disaster to Self-Kindness

At school I was kind of a big deal in the 800m track scene—at least in my own mind. Despite the fact that I had no intention of pursuing a professional career in running, and honestly didn't want to, I always felt incredibly anxious before any race. In fact, my anxiety got so intense that I would be physically sick before races. Probably why I have emetophobia now... but I digress! My mind would be consumed by negative thoughts: *'I'm terrible at this'*, *'Why am I here?'*, *'Everyone must think I'm a joke.'* This inner dialogue didn't just occupy my mind on the day of the event but often persisted for days and sometimes weeks before the race. I was overly critical of myself if I didn't finish in first place and worried about making a fool of myself. Little did I know at the time that this mindset was not helping me improve or enjoy the experience; it was actually holding me back!

More importantly, I spent years hating running and races because of the way I spoke to myself. It wasn't until years later—perhaps even a decade—that I realised how much better I would have felt if I had treated myself with the same kindness and compassion I would offer a friend in a similar situation. If I had approached each race as a learning experience, I might have enjoyed it (maybe!).

The funny thing now? I absolutely love running. It's my way to relieve stress and blow off the cobwebs. When I'm running longer distances and feeling the pain, I know now to encourage myself. If I had talked to myself the way I used to during races at school, I can assure you I wouldn't be running anymore.

So, before we dive into some practical tips for overcoming negative self-talk, let's have a look at whether positive self-talk really does help.

Brain Boost

One study investigated the role of self-talk in predicting anxiety about death and coping strategies in 354 adults living in Iran during the COVID-19 pandemic. They found a significant negative correlation between self-talk and death anxiety and emotional coping style—in other words, people who engaged in positive self-talk not only had less anxiety about death but had better strategies to cope with stress. (Damirchi, Mojarrad & Pireinaladin, 2020)

Lady Gaga, singer and actress, shares that in her journey toward healing, she has discovered that showing kindness to herself is the most powerful strategy.

Brain Boost

Another study investigated the effect of reciting a positive self-talk statement on performance anxiety. They asked students to read a self-affirming statement out loud prior to public speaking. They compared these students to a group that didn't use the statement. The students who read the positive statement reported feeling less anxious about their performance (Shadinger et al., 2020).

Let's look at how we can re-frame our inner voice:

Table 8.1 Examples of how to reframe negative self-talk into more constructive alternatives.

Negative Self-Talk	Positive Self-Talk
'I can't do it'	'I'll give it my best shot'
'I'm so stupid'	'I made a minor mistake'
'The stress is overwhelming'	'I have the strength to manage my stress'
'I'm such a failure'	'Everyone has setbacks, I will keep moving forward'
'I am not enough'	'I am more than enough'
'I'm not okay'	'I'll be fine'

Noting down some positive phrases and saying them aloud when you are feeling anxious—or, ideally, as a preventive technique when you feel yourself becoming anxious—can make you feel better and more in control of your worrying. Figure 8.2 provides some examples of phrases to write down and repeat. They might help you avoid judging yourself. Remember, your anxiety does not define you or your worth. Your thoughts and feelings are just the anxiety talking.

Just as a broken leg or an infected lung can heal, so can our anxiety.

Writing down some positive thoughts, experiences, affirmations and reflections may aid in shifting your mindset from self-critical to positive, contributing to long-lasting improvements in your mental wellbeing (Melhe et al., 2021). Consistency is key. We can rewire our neural pathways through repetitive thoughts and affirmations, creating new habits.

Figure 8.2 Speech bubbles filled with positive and motivating phrases.

Try it for yourself: *Positive Self-Talk Journal Prompts*

On a sheet of paper or in your journal, complete the following phrases:

I am proud of myself because ....
I am grateful for ....
Today I was helpful when ....
Something that made me smile today was ....
I learned from this mistake that ....
I was thankful for ....
I was a good friend when ....
I had fun when ....
I showed kindness today when ....
I am happy when ....

In The Boy, the Mole, the Fox and the Horse, *author and illustrator Charlie Mackesy reminds us that being kind to ourselves is just as important as being kind to others.*

Another tip to conclude this section is one I picked up from a friend—let's call her Mia.

Mia and her Inner Critic

Mia had battled for a long time with a pesky voice inside her head that she struggled to keep at bay. She often shared how overwhelming her anxiety could be—how it would spiral into overthinking, convincing her that everyone around her was annoyed with her and leading her to over-analyse every gesture. It left her feeling completely drained and she retreated further into herself. One day she was telling me about a time when her anxiety was particularly loud, and she couldn't take it anymore. She decided to name the voice in her head 'Maggy'. *'Now, when I catch myself spiralling into anxious thoughts'*, she said, *'I go, ah, that's just Maggy talking. Thanks for chiming in, but I'm not taking advice from you today.'* Giving the anxious voice a name helped her take a step back and regain perspective—the voice may show up from time to time, but it doesn't define her.

Despite not working in psychology, Mia taught me an important lesson that day that really stuck with me—a strategy I now share with others. As it happens, Mia's strategy is a popular psychological technique often used in therapy (for instance, Acceptance and Commitment Therapy) to help externalise one's anxious brain, creating distance between your thoughts and actions. By separating your thoughts from who you are, it is easier to respond more rationally and compassionately.

8.3 How Can Setting Goals Help Manage Anxiety?

It's not what happens to you, but how you react to it that matters.
Epictetus, Philosopher

Let's jump straight in with some more oversharing from yours truly:

The Sunday Scaries

For as long as I can remember, I have struggled with Sunday evenings. They've always brought a special kind of tension that I couldn't quite shake. Like clockwork, the Sunday scaries would turn up, uninvited, as the reality of the new week and looming responsibilities came into view. Perhaps some of you know what I'm babbling on about. In fact, it's relatively common, stemming from the anticipation of upcoming stress. For years, I accepted them as part of my week, but as time went on, I decided it was time to do something about them. One thing I discovered that helped me was writing down my goals for the week. Nothing was off-limits, whether it was putting on a load of laundry or finishing a work task, it would go on the checklist. Setting clear goals gave me a sense of control, allowing me to enjoy what I had left of my weekend without the dread of Monday and making the week ahead feel less overwhelming. I still rely on goal setting to this day to help kick my scaries to the curb!

Given my personal experience and the positive impact that setting goals has had on my life, I felt it deserved a spot in this book. Not to mention, it's been proven to be a powerful tool in reducing anxiety for a host of reasons. Let's break down a few of these:

- **Sense of purpose:** When we have something to work towards, we have a greater sense of meaning. This can help alleviate feelings of anxiety.
- **Sense of control:** Setting specific and achievable goals can help give you a sense of control in an otherwise chaotic world, helping reduce overwhelming feelings.
- **Routine:** Having some structure in our lives provides stability. This helps people prone to anxiety as it reduces uncertainty.

It doesn't matter how big the goals are, it's the action of working towards your objectives that is beneficial. Perhaps you could try practise something you've read in this book, such as a breathing exercise. Who knows what might help (everyone is different), but you'll never know if you don't try. The future you desire is closer than it may seem—progress comes one step at a time. The key is to keep moving forward, even when the goal feels painfully distant at present (this reflects Amber Lyon's teachings on perseverance; Lyon, 2024). As mentioned earlier, there's no 'one size fits all'. Try different things. Adopt, abandon, amend.

Practical Goal Setting

Research has shown that setting small achievable goals each week can be anxiety-reducing and helps people make positive changes in their life.

Your goals need to be: your choice, important to you, a little bit difficult to achieve/outside your comfort zone, realistic.

The SMART method is a powerful tool for setting and achieving goals (Ogbeiwi, 2021). Let's break it down so we can understand its significance and application.

In this example, I'm planning a goal to help improve my running.

1. **Specific:**
   - Be specific about what you want to achieve and why it is important to you. What do you need to do to achieve it? Saying 'I want to get fit' is too vague. Instead, a specific goal could be: 'I want to run 5k in 30 minutes by the end of the month.'
2. **Measurable:**
   - You need to be able to track your progress. This could be through measuring time, or distance. For example, if your goal is to run 5K, specify for how long you aim to run each week.
3. **Achievable:**
   - Being realistic is so important. Consider your current abilities and available resources. Obviously, you want to challenge yourself, but being overly ambitious can lead to you giving up early. Ensure that your goal is within reach—you are striving to go from A to B, not A to Z!
4. **Relevant**:
   - Ensure your goal aligns with your overall vision and aspirations—i.e. is it meaningful and will it contribute to your overall fulfilment and wellbeing?
5. **Time-Bound**:
   - Set a clear deadline for achieving your goal. You may even want to break your goal into smaller goals with deadlines to stay on course. For example, if your goal is to run that 5K, set a specific timeframe for completion.

Supplement your experience via the worksheet in Appendix D of the Additional Resources.

Let's look at an example to help you get started!

Evie has wanted to run more to improve her physical and mental health. She used to run 5Ks frequently but has struggled recently to do it in below 35 minutes. She wants a realistic and structured pathway to make this happen so decides to set herself a SMART goal.

Goal: I will run a 5K in 30 minutes within the next three months.

Specific: She wants to run 5K in a particular timeframe.

Measurable: This can be measured by whether she completes the 5K in under 30 minutes by the end of three months.

Achievable: Given her current level of fitness and time to train, this is a realistic goal.

Relevant: This goal aligns with her wish to improve her running performance and overall wellbeing.

Time-bound: The goal has a clear deadline of three months.

It's important to remember that falling off the wagon is part of the process—we're all human after all! I have veered off course more times than I can count. I'll give you an example which may sound somewhat familiar for you runners out there:

From Race-Ready to Couch Potato

After my best friend's mum lost her battle with cancer, I decided to jump on the half-marathon bandwagon and take part in my first race to raise money for Bowel Cancer UK. I started training about three months beforehand, as all the training plans tell you to. Big shock, I lost a lot of motivation with about a month to go when the cold, wet English weather set in and became the perfect excuse to snuggle up on the sofa and binge watch *Emily in Paris* (if you know, you know!). My carefully planned training schedule was no more. The old me would have just given up and skipped the race, but with a little self-compassion, I realised that it wasn't about being perfect but about persistence. I was able to re-focus my goals, put the skipped runs behind me, and get back into my training routine without any guilt! Guess what? I survived the half marathon and even found it somewhat enjoyable, which I never thought I'd say!

So, what's the takeaway? It's not about the slip ups; what matters is how we choose to respond. Instead of seeing it as a failure, we can view it as a valuable chance to learn more about ourselves using the self-compassion skills we've learned earlier! With that new and improved self-compassion, we can pick ourselves up, brush ourselves off, forgive the setback and continue moving forward.

Try it for yourself: *Set Your Own S.M.A.R.T. Goals*

Create your own SMART goals in your journal or on a piece of paper. If you like you can write this in pencil so that you can easily keep changing your goal posts. This is good and means you're pushing yourself!

Specific	*What specifically do you want to do?*
Measurable	*How will I track my progress?*
Achievable	*Is this realistic given my current resources?*
Realistic	*Why am I doing this? Is it meaningful to me?*
Time-bound	*When will I have this completed by?*

Supplement your experience via the worksheet in Appendix E of the Additional Resources.

8.4 7-Day Anxiety Buster Challenge

Try it out for a week and see how you feel. Enjoy the process and be gentle with yourself!

Day 1: Morning Mindful Breathing

- Begin the day with a simple, short mindfulness practice. Find a comfortable, quiet room and lie on your back with your knees bent (you can also do this exercise sitting upright on a chair if you prefer).
- Put one hand on your chest and the other on your stomach. Breathe in slowly through your nose until you can't take in any more air. Feel the air move through your body. Breathe out slowly through pursed lips (imagine you are sipping though a straw).
- Repeat the above steps a few times for best results. Practice for 5–10 minutes, setting a calm tone for the day ahead.

Day 2: Body Scan Meditation

- Find a quiet space where you can lie down comfortably, either on a yoga mat or your bed.
- Close your eyes and bring your awareness to your body. Start with your toes and gradually move your attention up through each part of your body, noticing any sensations without judgment.
- Spend a few breaths on each area, gently releasing tension and allowing yourself to relax deeper into the ground.
- Complete the body scan from head to toe. Feel a sense of relaxation and presence throughout your entire body.

Day 3: Mindful Eating

- Choose one meal today to eat mindfully. No screens or other distractions!
- Take a moment to appreciate the appearance and texture of the food you are eating.
- Eat slowly and relish each bite, attending to the flavour while chewing. Put your fork down, focusing on each mouthful. This will help slow down your eating.
- Observe how your body feels as you eat. Is it giving signals of hunger or satiety?
- Express gratitude for the nourishment of your meal.

Day 4: Nature Walk

- Set aside time to be outdoors today. As you walk, notice the colours, sounds and shapes of the world around you.
- Feel the ground beneath your feet with each step.
- Embrace the present and the beauty of nature.

Day 5: Journalling

- Take a few minutes to think of three things you're grateful for today.
- Write down why these are meaningful to you and how they impact your life.

Day 6: Goal Setting

- Set aside time to identify one short-term and one long-term goal.
- Write them down in your journal, making sure they are specific, measurable, achievable, relevant and time-bound (SMART).

Day 7: Reflection

- Set aside some time to reflect on your mindfulness journey this week. Have you noticed any changes in your energy, mood or wellbeing?
- Think about the mindfulness practices which you found most useful and consider how you could integrate them into your routine going forward.
- Give yourself a pat on the back! Celebrate the fact you're making self-care a priority!

Supplement your experience via the worksheet in Appendix F of the Additional Resources.

Reflect & Act: Putting it into Action

Reflect:
- Ask yourself: what do I need most right now?

Act:
- If it's emotional release, try journalling. If it's reassurance, try positive self-talk. If it's direction, try goal setting.

Key Takeaways

Before we move on, here's what to remember from this chapter:

- Journalling is a good way to express and process your emotions. It is free and can be practised anywhere and at any time.
- Our mind can be our biggest enemy when it comes to anxiety. Research has shown the benefits of positive self-talk, helping individuals to reframe challenges and build self-confidence.

- Practising positive inner dialogue can help nurture a supportive and compassionate mindset.
- Setting small, realistic goals can significantly help anxiety levels. Breaking down larger tasks into smaller, manageable steps helps to create a sense of control and accomplishment, reducing feelings of overwhelm.
- Creating a 7-day anxiety challenge is a good way to try out different techniques and see what works for you. It provides structure and allows you to track your progress, promoting a sense of achievement and motivation as you complete each day's activities.

Mission accomplished: Daily Tips Unlocked

Next stop: Now that you've mastered the tools to help yourself, it's time to turn your attention to your friends, family, estranged colleagues, etc. The next chapter will guide you in spotting signs of anxiety in others and help you avoid being a lemon when it comes to offering support. It's time to put your newfound expertise to good use and become the ultimate support hero for your people!

References

Brown, B. (2012). *Daring greatly: How the courage to be vulnerable transforms the way we live, love, parent, and lead.* Gotham Books.

Damirchi, E. S., Mojarrad, A., Pireinaladin, S. & Grjibovski, A. M. (2020). The role of self-talk in predicting death anxiety, obsessive-compulsive disorder, and coping strategies in the face of coronavirus disease (COVID-19). *Iranian Journal of Psychiatry, 15*(3), 182.

Lyon, A. (2024). *You are a magnet: Guiding principles for a magnetic and joyful life.* Hodder Catalyst.

Melhe, M. A., Salah, B. M. & Hayajneh, W. S. (2021). Impact of training on positive thinking for improving psychological hardiness and reducing academic stresses among academically-late students. *Kuram ve Uygulamada Egitim Bilimleri, 21*(3), 132–146.

Ogbeiwi, O. (2021). General concepts of goals and goal-setting in healthcare: A narrative review. *Journal of Management & Organization, 27*(2), 324–341.

Shadinger, D., Katsion, J., Myllykangas, S. & Case, D. (2020). The impact of a positive, self-talk statement on public speaking anxiety. *College Teaching, 68*(1), 5–11.

Smyth, J. M., Johnson, J. A., Auer, B. J., Lehman, E., Talamo, G. & Sciamanna, C. N. (2018). Online positive affect journaling in the improvement of mental distress and well-being in general medical patients with elevated anxiety symptoms: A preliminary randomized controlled trial. *JMIR Mental Health, 5*(4), e11290.

Anxiety Allies
How to Be the Best
Support Buddy

she was carrying something heavy –
I didn't know exactly what to do

Figure 9.1 A glimpse into my thoughts: a page from my personal journal.

Charlie Mackesy teaches us another important message in his book
The Boy, the Mole, the Fox and the Horse—*that we have no idea*
what someone is facing, and a touch of gentleness can go a long way.

> **GOAL:** To help you recognise the signs of anxiety in others and discover the best ways to support them.

You may be reading this book having sneakily avoided too many encounters with anxiety. Regardless, topping up your knowledge can help you spot the signs in others and know when and how to step in if required. Many people, especially men, are suffering in silence. There is still a lot of shame and embarrassment around speaking up about mental health. Let's change that. It just takes one conversation.

9.1 Spotting the Sneaky Signs of Anxiety

Sometimes the signs are different to what you expect. There are certain things that individuals with anxiety do that can come across as 'rude' to

DOI: 10.4324/9781003670117-10

others. Keep an eye out for the following, as any one of them *could* be an indication of something deeper and a combination is very likely to be a sign of someone struggling. Please try not to take it personally. It's not about you, in the nicest way possible!

1. **Lack of eye contact** → When someone feels anxious, this may affect their ability to maintain eye contact with someone. You may take this as someone being rude or uninterested in what you have to say, but sometimes it may be someone's anxiety talking.

2. **Making excuses** → People with anxiety often find social interactions difficult/anxiety-provoking (Voncken et al., 2006). They may cancel arrangements last minute or fail to show up. This can be incredibly aggravating but try to spare a moment to think why they have done this and how they must be feeling. It usually doesn't come from a bad place. At the time of making a plan, they are often very excited, but as the plan gets closer, it's harder for them not to doubt themselves and become overwhelmed by the thought.

3. **The so-called 'airing'** → People with anxiety may seem like they are ignoring your regular attempts to communicate via messages, etc. They may avoid these social interactions as they bring them a surge of negative symptoms.

4. **Agitated/'short'** →Anxiety can bring about varying symptoms, one of which makes them feel very on edge and constantly hypervigilant to the extent that, occasionally, they may snap at something that seems pretty minor (Wand & Draper, 2019).

5. **Not listening/concentrating** → Anxiety makes it difficult to process information and focus (Beck & Clark, 1997). This is obvious when you think about the bodily processes governing anxiety. We use up a lot of energy and resources when we are anxious as our body is working in 'overtime' essentially to cope with the unwanted and intrusive thoughts, making it difficult to think and concentrate. You may experience 'brain fog' or have difficulty planning or organising things. As discussed earlier, anxiety causes us to 'freeze' momentarily which hinders our ability to process information as quickly as we usually do. Anxious brains have a 'perceptual bias' towards threat, which influences the amount of information we can hold in our working memory (Feldborg et al., 2021). It's a double-edged sword as this slower processing speed may also foster feelings of anxiety. For example, anxiety may affect the ability to concentrate.

This can lead to missed deadlines, which worsens the anxiety. Therefore, you may perceive someone as being rude if they are not taking in what you are saying. However, this might be their anxiety. Be mindful of this.

Prince Harry has spoken about the importance of opening up about mental health. He's acknowledged that whilst it's often treated as a taboo, honest conversations and confiding in others can help break the stigma.

Now we've talked through some ways people with anxiety behave, let's take a look at what we can do today to ease the struggle. Whether it's a friend, colleague, family member—or that random person in your group chat—it's never too late or too small a gesture to reach out and offer support.

9.2 How to Help without Being a Helicopter

- **Check in:** Yes, this may seem obvious, but I think people underestimate the significance of a brief message. It doesn't need to be anything long or heavily thought out. It can just be a simple text, like *'Hey, just checking in to see how you're doing today'*. I hate to break it to you, but you probably should be doing this already. Checking in with friends is a must—sometimes, even a single short message can nudge the door open, if only slightly. And don't worry about what might be shared—just be there and listen. Most of the time, that's all someone really needs.

    I was really worried about Angie today… she just wasn't herself… quiet and withdrawn, like she was carrying something heavy… I didn't know exactly what to do, but I let her know I was there. I didn't try to fix it, I just listened. Slowly, she began to open up. For so long I was fearful of helping as I didn't think I had the answers… now I know I'm not meant to. Just showing up is enough…

    Me

- **Show compassion:** We talked earlier about self-compassion and how it is in fact easier to direct that compassion elsewhere. Well now's your chance! When we show compassion, we are creating a safe space for that person, promoting trust and openness. This is likely to make it easier for them to reach out and accept help when needed. Compassion is more important than ever—as we navigate a world littered with social pressures and mental health challenges. Let's challenge the stigma around vulnerability and practise kindness to ourselves and others.

- **Listen without judgement:** Give them your full attention and acknowledge their feelings. Yes, this means put down your phone for a whole five minutes (SHOCK!) and listen without distraction. The important thing is that they're talking about it and that takes a lot of courage.
- **Be patient and supportive:** Managing anxiety can be a slow process. It's important to remain supportive if they are not ready to talk yet. Knowing you're there can be enough. Remember, it's often the ones that you don't think suffer that suffer the most.

Why Not Try This?

Encourage your friend to think about who's in their support circle and how they might reach out to that person in times of need.

Someone who gets *me*

Someone I can talk to without needing to explain everything.

Name:
How to reach them:
When I might contact them:

Someone I can text or call when I'm spiralling

Someone I know will just reply and be there.

Name:
How to reach them:

- **Recommend healthy lifestyle habits:** Use the information and tools you've read about to help those around you.
- **Educate yourself:** If you've made it to this part of the book then you've already achieved this. Educating ourselves about anxiety goes a long way in better understanding and validating the experiences of others and how best to help.
- **Positive talk:** Explain to them how replacing negative thoughts with positive ones can decrease anxiety. Perhaps you could even use positive

self-talk yourself to demonstrate its credibility. Remind them that their anxiety does not define them.

- **Encourage professional help:** If their anxiety seems significant, you could suggest seeking professional help. Therapies like CBT and medications are effective for anxiety (Oparina et al., 2024). On World Mental Health Day, footballer Harry Kane shared an important message encouraging people to seek help if they're struggling—a reminder that vulnerability and strength often go hand in hand.

Let's have a look at a major concern for the younger generation—eco-anxiety—and how one girl helped her friend through it.

Eco Fears, Friendly Ears

The worry Anika felt for the current state of the climate quite literally kept her up at night. She couldn't understand why her peers weren't tearing their hair out with frustration and sadness. She was feeling overwhelmed and having trouble sleeping at night. Anika's friend, Josie, had noticed a change in Anika. She was skipping their weekly nights out and seemed more irritable than normal. Josie felt so help-less. One afternoon, Josie found Anika sitting alone in the University student union, staring blankly at the wall. She went over and asked if she was okay. Anika broke down in tears, 'It just feels like no matter what we do, it's never enough,' she exclaimed. 'The state of the cli-mate is getting worse, and no one seems to care or be doing anything about it.' Instead of brushing it off like most of Anika's other friends, Josie listened to her concerns—really listened, rather than just going through the motions. She empathised with her. 'I get it. It's terrifying', she said, 'but perhaps instead of trying to tackle it all at once—an overwhelming weight for any one person alone to take on—we start small?'

With a friend who truly validated her feelings, Anika felt relieved and ready to take small but meaningful steps forward. They signed up for a local tree-planting event and organised a clothes swap at school. Just channelling her anxiety into action made her feel so much bet-ter. Josie reminded Anika that it wasn't about big, earth-shattering gestures (excuse the pun!) or being perfect—it was about doing what you could, when you could. Slowly but surely, Anika felt like herself again. A weight had been lifted. Through the support of a good friend, she realised that while she couldn't do it all alone, she wasn't alone in trying either.

The people you surround yourself with are undeniably influential for who you are and where you are headed. Don't underestimate the power of your friends. For me, they are the best kind of therapy. Supportive, fiercely loyal, reassuring and, best of all, free! When I feel a bit down or anxious or overwhelmed, it's my friends that I turn to. A few back-and-forth messages or a natter in the park can be all I need to snap myself out of my funk. Sometimes, a little company can go a long way, and it's backed by science, no less. Spending time with the people you love can actually change your brain chemistry. Social interactions trigger the release of the body's 'love hormone', oxytocin, which strengthens bonds and enhances our ability to handle stress (Vuorisalmi, 2025). So next time you hang out with your loved ones, remember: you're not just having fun; you're investing in your brain. I'll caveat this, though, by saying it's about balance—sometimes, all you need is some personal space in your car singing at the top of your lungs to some cheesy power ballad!

Reflect & Act: Trusting Your Gut

Reflect:
- How would I want someone to support me if I were in their shoes? Think about how you'd want to be treated if you were feeling anxious. How would you want someone to show up for you? Use this as a guide for how to respond.

Act:
- Be a mirror of calmness. Focus on staying calm yourself. Slow your breathing and use soft, reassuring tones (this can be contagious).

Supplement your experience via the worksheet in Appendix G.

Key Takeaways

Before we move on, here's what to remember from this chapter:

- Sometimes when people are struggling with anxiety they can come across as rude. However, they're usually trying to manage intense and overwhelming feelings. Be patient.
- There are a few signs to look out for that might indicate someone is feeling anxious—for instance, lack of eye contact, making excuses, avoiding social occasions, appearing agitated, lack of concentration.
- Fear not, you can help by simply showing up. You can try a host of different things without coming across as overbearing.
- The most important thing is to be compassionate and avoid judgement. Everyone's on their own path, navigating their own internal and external environments. Be patient with yourself and those around you.
- Some of the time, a strong support network can help a person navigate their difficulties. However, it's important to know when it's gone too far. If their anxiety seems significant, you could suggest seeking professional help. There are many talking therapies and pharmacological support that are effective for anxiety.

Mission accomplished: You've Got Their Back

Next stop: Get ready to wrap things up with the key takeaways from the book. We'll revisit the important messages and see if we can make the essentials stick. Get ready for a stronger, calmer, and more resilient version of yourself.

References

Beck, A. T. & Clark, D. A. (1997). An information processing model of anxiety: Automatic and strategic processes. *Behaviour Research and Therapy, 35*(1), 49–58.

Feldborg, M., Lee, N. A., Hung, K., Peng, K. & Sui, J. (2021). Perceiving the self and emotions with an anxious mind: Evidence from an implicit perceptual task. *International Journal of Environmental Research and Public Health, 18*(22), 12096.

Oparina, E., Krekel, C. & Srisuma, S. (2024). *Talking therapy: Impacts of a nationwide mental health service in England* (No. 16839). IZA Discussion Papers. https://eprints.lse.ac.uk/126829/1/dp1982.pdf.

Voncken, M. J., Alden, L. E. & Bögels, S. M. (2006). Hiding anxiety versus acknowledgment of anxiety in social interaction: Relationship with social anxiety. *Behaviour Research and Therapy, 44*(11), 1673–1679.

Vuorisalmi, E. (2025). *The healing power of hormones: Harness dopamine, serotonin and oxytocin to unlock your best life*. Random House.

Wand, A. P. & Draper, B. (2019). Agitation. In *Primary care mental health in older people: A global perspective*, 331–347. Springer. https://doi.org/10.1007/978-3-030-10814-4_24.

The Bottom Line
Your Takeaway Toolbox

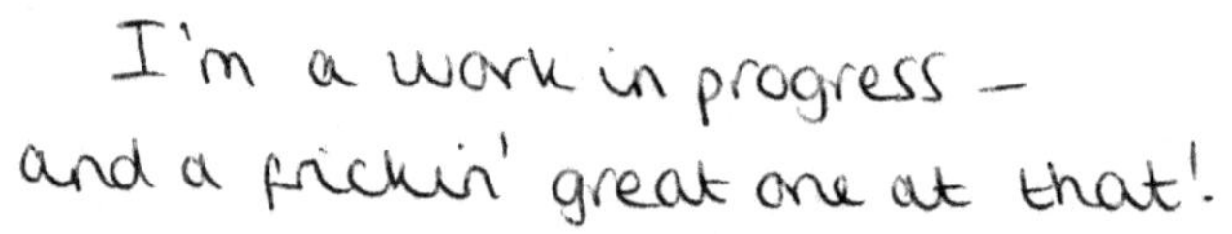

10

I'm a work in progress — and a frickin' great one at that!

Figure 10.1 A glimpse into my thoughts: a page from my personal journal.

Eleanor Roosevelt—author, humanitarian and former First Lady of the United States—observed that when we face our fears head on, we build strength and courage. Every frightening experience we survive proves that we can handle what's to come. She urges everyone to do the very thing they believe they cannot.

> **GOAL:** To review what you've learned and motivate you to move forward with newfound confidence and calm.

Congratulations reader, you've made it! As much as I would love you to use all the information and strategies tucked into these pages, I'm a realist and appreciate that life gets in the way. But if there's just one nugget of wisdom you take away from this book, I hope it's that no one is perfect, nor will someone live their life without ever experiencing anxiety in some capacity. I know—such a downer—but it's a universal human experience. Just like sadness and happiness are. Anxiety allows us to understand other bodily sensations and survive. Look on the bright side—it means you're never alone. Take all the real-life examples throughout this book, they provide a

DOI: 10.4324/9781003670117-11

glimpse of what people are going through every single day. Look up from your smartphone. It could be the guy opposite you on the tube drinking his overly bitter Pret coffee, or the cashier at your local Tesco, or even the smiley receptionist at your office. Next time you're out and about, be mindful of that. You never know what someone is going through. Being kind costs nothing and goes a long way. Especially in today's world. *You* have the power to make someone's day that little bit brighter.

It is important to understand that not every method or strategy for coping with anxiety will work for you, or those suffering around you. The key is, like most things in life, to find what works for your individual needs. Sometimes we don't try things because we think they're not suited to us or don't align with our capabilities, but you don't know until you try. Take what sticks, leave what doesn't—and come back any time you need a refresher.

Supplement your experience via the worksheet in Appendix H of the Additional Resources.

Taking to social media recently, actor Ryan Reynolds opened up about his longstanding struggle with anxiety, which often leads him to overthink and bite off more than he can chew. He reassured others experiencing similar feelings that they are not alone.

To summarise some of the main points:

- Anxiety is a natural response to stress or potential danger. Anxiety experienced on an occasional basis is normal, but when excessive or chronic, it can be debilitating.
- There are different types of anxiety, including (but not limited to) generalised anxiety, social anxiety, panic attacks and phobias.
- The brain plays a crucial role in the regulation of anxiety. The amygdala is responsible for processing emotions, particularly fear. When it detects a threat, it initiates the fight or flight response which prepares the body to respond. An overactive amygdala is associated with elevated anxiety levels.
- Psychodynamic, behavioural and cognitive theories are three big psychological theories that help explain anxiety. They highlight the role of childhood experiences, conditioning and the interaction of our thoughts, feelings, and behaviours in the development and maintenance of anxiety.

- Anxiety impacts both the mind and body (greedy, isn't it!). You may experience psychological symptoms, such as racing thoughts or difficulty concentrating, and/or physical symptoms, such as increased heartrate and sleep issues.
- Adolescence is a particularly important time for brain development. During this time, the amygdala is very active and hormonal levels are rising, making us more sensitive to emotional stimuli. Our search for belonging, connection (both romantic and platonic) and independence catapult the susceptibility to anxiety to a new high. Adding the current economic and environmental state of the world to the mix makes for a rather unfair entrance to adulthood in my eyes. Can I get a refund?!
- There are many small changes we can make to our daily lives which may help to reduce anxiety (finally, some good news!). Diet, exercise, sleep and screen use all have an impact. Everyone is different and what helps will depend on what is specific to the individual among a wide range of factors. It's unlikely that a single thing will dissolve anxiety, particularly for those who experience it on a severe scale. In such cases, eating less refined sugar is unlikely to help in isolation. However, a combination of things may help.
- Breathing and guided imagery exercises, such as belly breathing and short body scans, can help calm the nervous system and synchronise the mind and body. These are all quick and simple, and backed by science, meaning there's no excuse for not trying at least one of them out!
- There are other avenues to explore if the exercises above haven't clicked just yet. Journalling can be good for processing emotions and gaining clarity amidst the chaos. Positive self-talk can help nurture a supportive and compassionate mindset. Setting small goals (think SMART!) can help build a sense of control and reduce the noise. Why not create your own 7-day anxiety challenge so you can try out different techniques and see what fits?
- It's important to look out for others who might be struggling. We all need someone to lean on sometimes. There are several things to be aware of, which will make your ability to help in a timely manner more effective! The overriding message—be present, compassionate and avoid judgement.
- **It's okay not to be okay.** Many people have struggled, and will struggle, with their mental health. Speaking up and sharing experiences can help reduce the stigma and build a more compassionate society.

- You're not meant to have it all figured out! We are only human after all. Slow down a bit, check in with yourself (and others!) and consume mindfully (both physically and virtually).

Man sacrifices his health in order to make money. Then he sacrifices money to recuperate his health. And then he is so anxious about the future that he does not enjoy the present; the result being that he does not live in the present or the future; he lives as if he is never going to die, and then dies having never really lived.

often attributed to the Dalai Lama, Spiritual Leader

Reflect & Act: Onwards and Upwards

Reflect:
- Take a moment to think about what stood out for you most from your reading. Is there anything you could start right now? Is there anything you want to revisit later down the line?

Act:
- I think it's time to set yourself a challenge. This week, let's try one breathing exercise, saying one kind thing to yourself and listening to a friend without judging. Remember, it doesn't need to be big. Small and steady wins the race!

Have you ever seen a reel or listened to a podcast where an older individual has been asked, 'What would you tell your younger self if you had the chance?' A large proportion of the answers I've heard to date are along the lines of 'I would tell my younger self not to worry, that everything's going to be okay'. I know we don't know that it is in fact going to be okay, but if we could just channel even a small amount of our anxious energy into some-thing more constructive, I can bet my right arm it'd be used for the better.

There's this one clip from a film called *Passenger*. The famous bartender scene. Some of you may know it. It follows an exchange between a bar-tender, Arthur, and a man named Jim, who asks the bartender to bestow some words of wisdom on him. Arthur replies saying that he suspected Jim wasn't where he thought he should be. He went on to say that even if Jim *were* in the place he thought he should be, he bet he'd still feel the same way. The point he was making is that if you get too caught up in where you'd rather be, you'll miss out on what's right in front of you. Arthur advises Jim to take a step back from what he cannot control and start living. This powerful exchange helped Jim to switch his inner narrative from loss to presence. Its sentiment extends far beyond a mere exchange in a film scene.

So, to reiterate the above in a shockingly audacious manner: Sing out loud. Order that pasta. Dance like no one's watching. Appreciate the small things. Hug that bit stronger. Kiss that bit more passionately. Smile because you can. Worry less (unless Boris Johnson is back in office—now that really is shared trauma and it's time to spiral together). In all seriousness, spread your body out (think power pose) and take up space in the world, unapologetically. As much as social media would want you to believe otherwise, self-care isn't about drinking matcha and going to sleep early! It's about saying no to things you don't want to do, just because you can, asking for support when you need it, and chasing what is *your* happy!

Before we finish, I want to tell you about a time when anxiety felt like it was in charge—and how I started to take that power back.

A Small Win in Outsmarting Anxiety

I still remember the morning when my anxiety felt completely overwhelming. I was lying in bed, heart pounding, mind racing through a list of 'what-ifs'. I was convinced this panic would never end. But this time, instead of trying to push the feelings away, I did something different: I sat up, placed my hand on my chest, and took slow, deep breaths, counting to four each time. I whispered to myself, *'My thoughts don't define me, and this moment will pass.'* It wasn't an instant fix, but it was the catalyst of a new way of thinking about myself and the words I use inside my mind.

Anxiety hasn't disappeared from my life—it still shows up in unexpected ways and catches me off guard. What matters is that I keep trying, despite the obstacles in front of me. Every time you stand back up, you are stronger. Celebrating the small things—getting out of bed on a tough day or simply weathering the storm—is a testament to your strength and resilience.

Writing this book has been part of my own journey towards understanding and contentment. I've surprised myself with my own strength and willpower, as I hope you will too as you edge closer to realising what your own mind is capable of. As you close these final pages, I want you to know that your experience matters. It's completely human to be scared, confused or drained. But you have time and capacity to grow.

I'm a work in progress, and a frickin' great one at that! I know there will be days when it creeps up on me, but I know now that I'm never alone. I know I can keep going. I know I am enough…

Me

Finally (and I really mean it this time!), I hope this book has left you in a better place then it found you. I'll leave you now with one of my favourite quotes, which you may recall reading in the initial pages of the book. Perhaps now it has more meaning than it did before?

You can't control the wind, but you can adjust your sails.
Kristen Proby, *New York Times* bestselling author

It's basically saying that, like the wind, there are things in life we cannot control no matter how hard we try. Challenges and 'curve balls' are an inevitable part of life. We all have them; it's just a matter of when. Often the things that are more challenging are the things that make us stronger (I digress!). Though we cannot control some things, we can find new ways to steer us through certain obstacles that present themselves along our journey. In other words, we may not be able to control everything that happens to us, but we can control how we respond.

Remember, you're the captain of your ship!

Resources and Further Reading

GAD-7 Questionnaire and NHS Questionnaire

The Generalized Anxiety Disorder 7-item scale (GAD-7; Spitzer et al., 2006) is a widely used tool to screen for anxiety. In 2010, Pfizer made the GAD-7 available at no charge. You can download the free questionnaire directly from the Anxiety & Depression Association of America (ADAA), or find it online—for instance, via Patient.info.

Please be mindful that whilst a high score *may* suggest significant anxiety, it is not enough to provide a clinical diagnosis. If you're concerned about your mental health, please seek professional help. A mental health professional will assess you and recommend appropriate treatment. Remember, you don't have to struggle in silence.

You can also find the **'Check my emotional and mental wellbeing'** questionnaire created by the NHS which is an online self-assessment tool to help people understand their mental health. It consists of questions about your recent feelings and behaviours to provide an overview of your mental health and then uses the information to recommend next steps, if required.

Here is a general pathway to access it:

1. Visit the NHS website.
2. Find the mental health section.
3. Navigate to self-assessment tools or emotional wellbeing questionnaires.

Podcasts, Pages and People that Help

Below are some additional avenues of support and guidance which may be helpful. There is a lot of noise out there, and it can be hard to know who to trust. These are some of the voices that I've found helpful, educated and grounded—whether in need of some real talk about mental health or inspiration for living well. I've grouped them into podcasts and social media pages to keep things easy.

= Personal Favourite

Podcasts

Stompcast—Dr Alex George
A walk-and-talk podcast that gets guests moving and opening up about mental health, life challenges and everything in between.

I Did a Runner—Josh Patterson
Honest conversations about mental health and the powerful role of movement in managing anxiety and building resilience.

Therapy for Black Girls—Dr Joy Harden Bradford
Smart, supportive and empowering discussions around mental health, identity and healing.

Feel Better, Live More—Dr Rangan Chatterjee
Deep dives into mental and physical health with leading experts—practical, uplifting and always insightful.

Terrible, Thanks for Asking—Nora McInerny
Real stories about pain, healing and resilience shared with humour and honesty.

High Performance—Jake Humphrey
Conversations with high achievers across multiple fields exploring the mindsets and habits that drive lasting success.

How to Fail—Elizabeth Day*
Guests are asked to provide three significant failures in their lives and share the lessons they've learnt as a result. Re-invents the notion of 'failure' into one of growth and resilience. Deeply personal and effortless funny. A must-listen!

The Wellness Scoop—Ella Mills & Rhiannon Lambert*
A myth-busting podcast about nutrition, wellbeing and the science behind healthy living. I turn to it when I want clear, science-backed wellness advice delivered in a friendly and unintimidating manner.

Social Media Pages Worth a Follow

@dralexgeorge—Dr Alex George
Mental health advocate and youth ambassador sharing accessible, real-world wellbeing tips.

@emthenutritionist—Emily English
Nutritional advice that's easy to digest (pun intended) and genuinely helpful.

@nicolesneuroscience—Dr Nicole Vignola
Bite-sized brain science with practical strategies for focus, memory and managing stress.

@healthymindpsychologyuk—Dr Amber Johnston
Thoughtful psychology content with a compassionate, trauma-informed lens.

@anxietycoach
Tips and affirmations specifically for managing anxiety and overwhelm.

@the.holistic.psychologist
Dr. Nicole LePera shares practical tools for healing trauma and improving mental wellness.

@nedratawwab
Therapist Nedra offers clear, compassionate advice on boundaries, anxiety and self-care.

@youngmindsuk
Youth mental health charity sharing resources, stories and campaigns.

@mindcharity
Mind UK charity offers mental health advice and raises awareness.

@sambentley*
For uplifting news that cuts through all the negativity - it never fails to lift my spirits!

Books

Martha Beck, *Beyond Anxiety*
Insightful guidance on understanding and moving beyond anxiety.

Catherine Pittman and Elizabeth Karle, *Anxiety, Rewire Your Anxious Brain: How to Use the Neuroscience of Fear to End Anxiety, Panic, and Worry*
A science-based approach to calming anxiety through brain rewiring.

Alicia Clark, *Hack Your Anxiety*
Practical strategies to take control and reduce anxiety in daily life.

Ian Tuhovsky, *Rewiring the Anxious Brain: Conquer Worry and Anxiety, Reduce Stress, Stop Overthinking, and Calm Your Mind with Proven Strategies*
Tools to retrain your brain and ease anxious thoughts.

Christopher Willard, *Mindfulness for Teen Anxiety: A Workbook for Overcoming Anxiety at Home, at School, and Everywhere Else*
Hands-on exercises for teens to manage anxiety through mindfulness.

Regine Galanti, *Anxiety Relief for Teens: Essential CBT Skills and Mindfulness Practices to Overcome Anxiety and* Stress
CBT-based techniques tailored for teenagers.

Edmund J. Bourne, *The Anxiety and Phobia Workbook*
Practical guide with exercises and coping strategies.

David D. Burns, *Feeling Good: The New Mood Therapy* by
Classic CBT techniques for anxiety and depression.

Barry McDonagh, *Dare*
A modern approach to overcoming anxiety and panic attacks.

Charlie Mackesy, *The Boy, the Mole, the Fox and the Horse**
A beautifully illustrated and heartwarming story of friendship, vulnerability and hope through the conversations of unlikely companions.

Jonathan Haidt, *The Anxious Generation**
Explores how the shift from free-play childhood to one that is largely 'phone-based' has 'rewired' brains and contributed to a surge in mental health problems, such as anxiety and depression. Fascinating and enlightening!

129

Apps

Headspace
Guided meditation and mindfulness for stress and anxiety.

Calm*
Meditation, sleep stories, and relaxation tools.

WorryTree
A CBT-based app to help manage worry and anxiety.

Moodpath
Mental health assessment and tracking tool.

Professional Organisations and Support Groups

Support Services/Helplines

NHS Direct
111
http://www.nhsdirect.nhs.uk/

The Samaritans
116 123 (or text 07725 909090)
jo@samaritans.org

SANEline
0300 304 7000
http://www.sane.org.uk/home

C.A.L.L (helpline for Wales)
0800 132 737 (or text 81066)
http://www.callhelpline.org.uk/

No Panic
0300 772 9844
sarah@nopanic.org.uk

Muslim Youth Helpline
0808 808 2008
help@myh.org.uk

Talking Therapy

Find a therapist with Better Health—https://betterhelp.com
NHS Talking Therapies Service—https://www.nhs.uk/service-search/mental-health/find-an-nhs-talking-therapies-service

Support Groups

Anxiety UK
Mind (side by side forum; blogs and stories; relaxation video)
Rethink Mental Illness
The Mix (13–25 year olds)
SANE

Additional Resources

Every Mind Matters: self-help CBT techniques
NHS audio guides: https://www.nhs.uk/mental-health/self-help/guides-tools-and-activities/mental-wellbeing-audio-guides/

Reference

Spitzer, R. L., Kroenke, K., Williams, J. B. & Löwe, B. (2006). A brief measure for assessing generalized anxiety disorder: The GAD-7. Archives of internal medicine, *166*(10), 1092–1097.

Appendices

Appendix A: My CBT Hot Cross Bun

Now you try: Use this worksheet to map out a real situation and get a better understanding about how your thoughts, feelings, and behaviours are all connected. This can help you notice your own patterns and begin to shift the unhelpful parts.

Date/Time: _____

Situation	What was happening? Where were you? Who was present?
Thoughts	What was going through your mind?
Emotions	How did you feel? How many emotions can you name? Rate the severity (0–10).
Physical sensations	How did your body react?
Behaviours	What did you do next? Did you say or do anything? Did you avoid something?
Patterns	Have you felt this way before? Does anything in particular stand out in the way you react to similar situations?
What might help?	Is there one thing you could try differently? A more realistic or compassionate thought, a calming strategy, or some positive self-talk?

Appendix B: My Coping Strategies Toolkit

Now you try: Use this worksheet to map out some ideas that work for you.

Category	Coping Strategy
Physical	e.g. get outside, go for a stroll, body stretch
Social	e.g. call a friend, cuddle a pet
Creative	e.g. draw, bake, knit
Calming	e.g. deep breathing, take a bath
Digital platforms	e.g. Use Calm app, listen to Headspace
Solution-focused	e.g. write a to-do list, prioritise tasks

Appendix C: Self-Compassion Letter

Now you try: Use this worksheet to help you to be more accepting of your distress, express non-judgement, and direct warmth to you.

There's no right way to do it. Take your time and listen to yourself. It's ok to go back, cross things out, or change it entirely if you want to.

1. Greet yourself. For example, *'Dear Amy'* or *'Dear me'*. Whatever feels right.
2. Name the problem that you are currently, or have previously, been struggling with. For example, *'I know you've been struggling with ....'*
3. Acknowledge how this made you feel.
4. Outline what you have done to cope—even if it didn't feel effective at the time.
5. Jot down what you would like to do to manage this better in the future. What setbacks or fears might crop up in your journey?
6. Read the letter back to yourself. Silently or out loud—up to you!

Appendix D: My Values & Vision

Now you try: Use this worksheet to help you explore what's truly important to you.

My top 5 values
(Write your own, e.g. kindness, adventure, family, independence, helping others).

1. _____
2. _____
3. _____
4. _____
5. _____

Now write down how you'd like to live in line with your values for each area of your life.

Life Area	What this looks like
Home	e.g. create a quiet space where I can relax, spend time with my family
Work/School	e.g. be creative in my projects
Relationships	e.g. surround myself with kind people, be a compassionate listener
The World	e.g. speaking up against injustice, reducing waste, donating to charity, volunteering

Vision Board

If I were living in line with my values, what would my life look like?

Let your creative juices flow. Doodle, stick in pictures, or write some short sentences.

Appendix E: My Goals

Now you try: Use this worksheet to set meaningful goals that feel realistic and track your progress!

My Goal (What I want to achieve):	
Why this matters to me:	
What steps will help me get there?	Step 1: _____ Step 2: _____ Step 3: _____
What obstacles might get in my way?	
My reward for completing it:	

Appendix F: My Anxiety Tracker

Now you try: Use this worksheet to help you track patterns in your anxiety over time. Rate your anxiety from 0 (none) to 10 (maximum). Jot down any thoughts that come up.

Day	Anxiety Rating 0–10	What is happening?	Did anything help?
Monday			
Tuesday			
Wednesday			
Thursday			
Friday			
Saturday			
Sunday			

Appendix G: My Circle of Support

Now you try: Use this worksheet to help identify the people (or pets/services) who are in your corner! Use the inner circles for those closest to you and outer ones for less frequent support.

Imagine *You* are in the very centre (bullseye!). The next layer out will be those you can turn to at any time (e.g. Mum, best friend, dog).

The next layer is those who are supportive and comforting to you, but not necessarily always available or your first point of call (e.g. cousin, therapist).

The outer layer is those who you can reach out to when needed but aren't necessarily always available to you (e.g. GP, online forum).

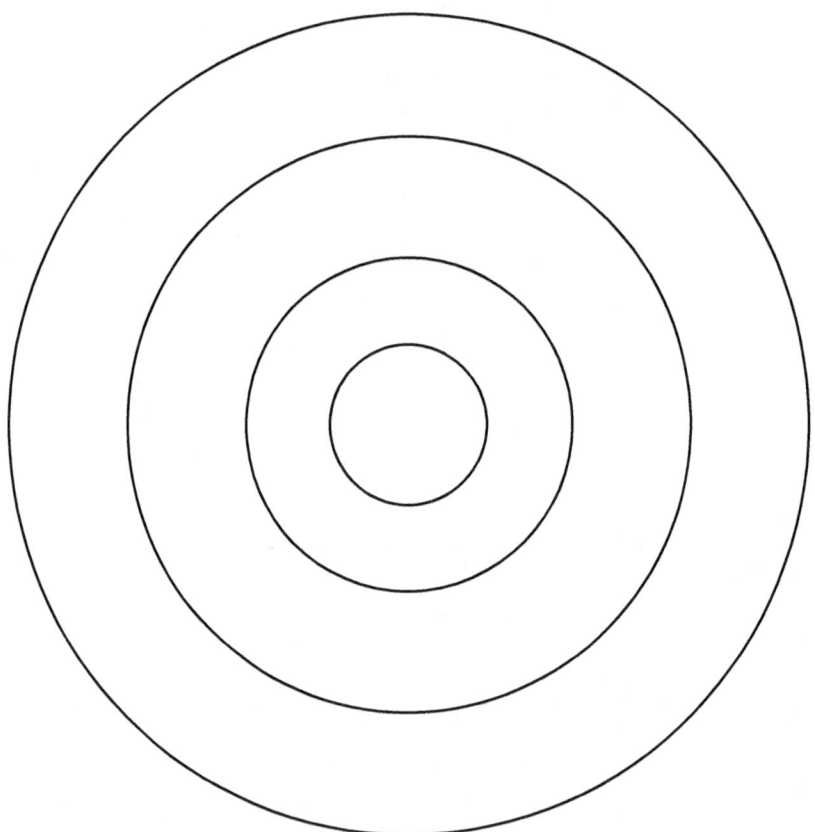

Copyright material from Lily Felton (2026), *Outsmart Anxiety*, Routledge

Appendix H: My Coping Plan

Now you try: Use this worksheet to help you in moments when anxiety starts to creep in.

My early signs of stress

(e.g. sweating, racing heart, withdrawal)

Safe people I can reach out to

Name and contact information (e.g. friend, family member, teacher)

Places where I feel safe, relaxed

(e.g. home, bedroom, park, school)

Go-to strategies that work

(e.g. breathing exercises, movement, journalling, goal setting, creativity)

Things that *don't* usually help

(e.g. processed food, doom-scrolling, avoiding situations)

One thing I need to remind myself of daily

(e.g. personal affirmation or quote that calms and empowers me)

Index

For Product Safety Concerns and Information please contact our EU
representative GPSR@taylorandfrancis.com
Taylor & Francis Verlag GmbH, Kaufingerstraße 24, 80331 München, Germany

www.ingramcontent.com/pod-product-compliance
Lightning Source LLC
Chambersburg PA
CBHW070423290526
45791CB00005B/1817